All I Need Is In God's Word

All I Need Is In God's Word

A Philosophical Option In Facing and
Dealing with the Problematic
Circumstances of Life

Dr. Billy Blackmon

Although the author has made every effort to ensure that the information in this book was correct at the time of first publication, the author does not assume and hereby disclaims any liability to any party for any loss, damage, or disruption caused by errors or omissions, whether such errors or omissions result from negligence, accident, or any other cause.

Copyright © 2023 by Billy Blackmon

All rights reserved. No part of this book may be reproduced or transmitted in any form or by any means, electronic or mechanical, including photocopying, recording, or any information storage and retrieval system, without permission in writing from the author.

ISBN: 978-1-6653-0522-8

This ISBN is the property of BookLogix for the express purpose of sales and distribution of this title. The content of this book is the property of the copyright holder only. BookLogix does not hold any ownership of the content of this book and is not liable in any way for the materials contained within. The views and opinions expressed in this book are the property of the Author/Copyright holder, and do not necessarily reflect those of BookLogix.

Library of Congress Control Number: 2023900187

⊚This paper meets the requirements of ANSI/NISO Z39.48-1992 (Permanence of Paper)

Scripture quotations marked "AMP" are from the Amplified Bible, copyright © 2015 by The Lockman Foundation, La Habra, CA 90631. All rights reserved. For Permission To quote information visit http://www.lockman.org/. Scripture quotations marked "NASB" are taken from the New American Standard Bible®, Copyright © 1960, 1962, 1963, 1968, 1971, 1972, 1973, 1975, 1977, 1995 by The Lockman Foundation. Used by permission. Scripture quotations marked "KJV" are taken from the Holy Bible, King James Version (Public Domain). Scripture quotations marked "NIV" are taken from the Holy Bible, New International Version®, NIV®. Copyright © 1973, 1978, 1984, 2011 by Biblica, Inc.™ Used by permission of Zondervan. All rights reserved worldwide.

012623

CONTENTS

Preface		vii
1 —	The Beginning	1
2 —	Getting Started	9
3 —	Habits	17
4 —	Going Forward	27
5 —	The Struggle	33
6 —	Back Again	41
7 —	Going Forward Again	51
8 —	Same Folk	61
9 —	What To Do, What To Do	77
10 —	From Here To There	87
11 —	The Way It Was	97
12 —	The Light	105
13 —	Figuring It Out	115
14 —	The Found Answer	125
15 —	Application	139
16 —	Renewal	151

17 — All-Inclusive	169
18 — Overpowering Confusion	177
19 — The End Results	185
20 — Getting It	197
21 — Hard But Well Worth It	211
Acknowledgments	231

PREFACE

I have written this book to share with the world my personal experiences that culminated exclusively in the certainty of truth, that everything I need to know for the fulfillment of life is in God's Word. It is my prayer to God that the person who reads the detailed catalogs of my story will receive the message of it as certified truth. May God bless the reader with an inspiration of hope and power as they seek the Lord for answers and direction, for all that a person needs is there—it's in the Word!

Now, initially and up front, I must make a few straightforward, honest, candid confessions, since they say "honest confession is good for the soul." I have used poetic license to my advantage for writing purposes and effects. I openly admit that I have prevaricated some issues to make the text more interesting. Some of the events have also been embellished to heighten and enhance the details of certain accounts. While I'm in confession mode, I want to make it known that there may also have been a merging of occurrences that brought about the same results.

Many years ago, when I was in college, at the encouragement of an English language professor, I sought to increase my vocabulary and improve my mastery of my native tongue. In doing so, I experienced some growing pains in my relationships. My friends and "home boys" were not communicating with me as they had in the past. In fact, I experienced a period of isolation as if I had an incurable communicable disease. When I discussed the matter with a friend, his honesty opened my eyes to a reality I was not aware of. He said to me (quoting him verbatim to the best of my recollection), "[Expletive] Bill Earl, don't nobody know the [expletive] you're saying using all those big words. Save them when you write a book, then whoever reads it can look them up in a [expletive] dictionary. When you talk to us, we don't have a dictionary!"

With the memory of the crude and harsh prophetic words (of which he or I probably never felt would come to pass) of my friend, I now write a book and will acquiesce to his advice. In writing this book, I have utilized and inserted words of my gathered collecting in the English language. Therefore, if there be any who come across a word or words that present a hardship in understanding, get a dictionary and look up the word—all you need to know is there, it's in the dictionary!

I pray that God will bless everyone who reads the word of this amateur and unprofessional writer. I can say with certainty in the faith of my encounters, God will bless that person's efforts. Please be cognitive of the fact that it is not a "rush order fix" to your situation in life, but I hope the reader will be blessed with overcoming power. I do not try to claim any recognition but give glory to God. The few I have witnessed to the way of winning their victories over Satan have told me of their personal success. So, please be patient and wait on the Lord! You will find yourself growing in the Lord, in Word and deed. You'll be able to witness and agree with the Prophet Isaiah as he proclaims in Isaiah 40:31 (AMP), "But those who wait for the Lord—who expects, look for and hope in Him—shall change and renew their strength and power; they shall lift their wings and mount up [close to God] as eagles [mount up to the sun]; they shall run and not be weary; they shall walk and not faint or become tired."

God does not want us to be ignorant and has given us directive in His Word (the Bible). Seek Him, seek His way, seek Him in the Bible. It's there—all we need to know is in His Word!

1
THE BEGINNING

I am the youngest of seven children born to Roosevelt Sr. and Maggie Blackmon. I have made the assessment that our mother and father were looking for the perfect child, and after I came along, there was no need to try for another. However, my siblings have a somewhat different opinion. As the youngest child, my mother, when introducing me, would often refer to me as "my baby." I detested the reference and would respectably and gently protest the usage; I was smart enough not to demand a stoppage altogether. My mother didn't play that, and I knew it wouldn't be tolerated. I learned to live with it and, at the same time, avoid a confrontation between a strap and my behind.

I don't know who taught me the alphabet or how to count, whether it was my parents or a sibling. Whoever did it posed a great imposition on me: Whenever we had company, invariably I would be called upon and hear my mother say, "Come on, baby, and say your ABCs (or "count") for us." In the public setting, from my mother's mouth to the world's ears, where I was concerned, it was "my baby." I'm sure our visitors were tired of what "my baby" could do, as was I. Our company was too gracious to voice an objection, and I wasn't brave or dumb enough to raise an objection, so we all tolerated the onslaught.

Life is filled with convoluted complexities. It was so with my mother calling me "my baby" when I was a child. As a youth, I hated it with a passion when the term was used so frequently toward me by my mother. However, as time progressed, I realized I was becoming an "old man," and the "baby" terminology from my mother was welcomed and sounded pretty good. In fact, in later years, I asked my mother why she stopped referring to me as "my baby."

I was born in Malvern, Arkansas ("God's Country"). My parents, in my childish mind and opinion, were the two dullest people in town. I can truthfully say that, other than one isolated incident, I never heard either of my parents use a word of profanity, unless they were directly quoting the words of someone else. The one incident I can remember is the time when my mother lost it and let anger get the best of her. She blurted out, "Dammit, the hell!" It was hilarious to my young ears, but I was smart enough not to laugh out loud, for obvious reasons. I wanted to pull my dear mother aside and say to her, "Listen, Mama, if you're going to do it, this is how you say it!"

My home environment was actionless. My parents did none of the cool things—they didn't smoke, drink, cuss, or gamble—they were just two old, dull folks (in their forties). I had to go to the homes of neighboring friends to witness "the happenings." Some of my friends had parents who knew how to live, in the mind of this child's eyes, exciting and electrifying lives. It was at my neighbors' houses that I could find the fascinations of smoking, drinking, and cussing. It was in these houses I could steal a cigarette or pick up a discarded butt and occasionally enjoy the bitter or burning effects of an alcoholic beverage. I would only have to go to the next block to witness and be entrenched with some more smoking, drinking, cussing, and watching money exchanged in chances of gambling exercises. I couldn't get excitement at home, but I was grateful to know that "good times were near me." Oh yes, home was boring, but there was plenty of fun stimulation to be found just over the horizon.

My parents made sure their children attended Sunday School, Morning Worship Services and Evening Services, and BTU (Baptist Training Union). We were definitely "churched" growing up in a mundane environment. It was not so then, but now, all grown, I am grateful for parents who made sure their children were brought up to know the Lord.

When I was a small child, I vividly remember looking at a family Bible (the really big one) that could be seen on the coffee table of every home that a person was allowed to enter. In the simplicity of my innocent mind, I thought it would take a lifetime to read such a humongous book. After I learned to read, I thought now was the best time to start. I even began carrying a Bible around with me. This Bible was smaller in size and was the entire Bible, so I don't know why I never reasoned about the size of it. I suppose I was just mesmerized by the size and thought of the bigger edition. I wanted to read it before I left this world, and I needed all this time to get it done.

You would have thought I received encouragement from adults, but to the contrary, I was ridiculed and lambasted by grown-ups. When I think on these times, I can't recall ever been teased by my peers for carrying my Bible. However, I was often (more times than I care to remember) chastised by Christians (I'd rather refer to them as "church folk") to "put that Bible down and play like other children." They would do this even when they saw me playing with other children. I would lay my Bible down in a safe place, play, and then pick the Bible up when I was finished. I was hurt by their derision. Their words were damaging and detrimental, to say the least, but through it all, I learned there is a God!

My grandmother, who was visiting from Detroit, Michigan, helped me tremendously during this unsettled time of my life. I don't know if my grandmother knew of the verbal abuse I was going through or if it was her wisdom and/or womanly intuition that was in operation. However, God touched this dear woman to give me a small, pocket-size copy of the Gideon New Testament with the Psalms. I remember my grandmother's words to me: "Grandmother always want you to read the Bible. Take this and keep it in your pocket so people won't make fun of you."

It was just the thing I needed at this most critical time. I have never forgotten that special, intimate incident that spurred an inspiration from my grandmother, something I have never received from any other human being. Her love and comforting favor may have been the commencement of my inspiration to want to preach. I cannot declare when the desire came, and can't say it was then, but I do know it was effectual in her grandson's life.

In those days, in Malvern ("God's Country"), we had many tent revivals by Black and White Pentecostal Churches. I have been told by my parents and siblings that I would cry and tell them I wanted to go on stage and preach. I have often wondered what would have happened if they had allowed me to go up (probably burst out in tears, crying). I was told by an aunt of my boyhood preaching antics in the yard, and according to her, I "sounded pretty good." I do remember that, as children, we would "play church," and ironically, I was always the preacher. Even when I advanced in school, the class clowns, of which I was a standing member, would sometimes play church and there, too, I was always the preacher. I have to make this declaration: If I did want to preach as a child, it was quenched as I got older in my teen years.

Upon becoming an adult, I have, many times, ruminated over my life and growing up. Thinking back on those times, I can now see that preaching may have been my destiny, even in jest. After all, the Bible does firmly declare that God's ways are not our ways and His ways are as high above our ways as the heavens are above the earth.

I was educated in the Malvern ("God's Country") public school system. I was somewhat talkative and rambunctious during my elementary and high school years. I admit my conduct was less than what would be expected and/or desired. I suppose it was tolerated by my teachers and not reported to my parents because I would always have homework assignments finished on time and I did well on my tests. I was blessed to be able to read and process knowledge with an ease that made me the envy of my peers. I was able to hang out with my friends and still manage to turn in my homework and make good grades. My friends would frequently ask me how I was able to accomplish all this and hang out with them. I was accused of staying up into the early morning hours doing my homework and studying after I got home from being out with them. One friend told me a group of them followed me home one night to see if there was a light in my room to prove I studied when I got home. This friend told me he wasn't supposed to tell me, but they then learned I wasn't doing what they accused me of. All I can say and testify to is that God blessed me mentally and I did not have to do a great deal of studying to maintain good grades.

Now, however, looking back on my fractious conduct, I can offer a reasonable summation for my acting out. All through my school experience, I was invariably compared to one of my older siblings. I often heard from my teachers, "You're (sibling's name) brother, he/she didn't act like this." I honestly feel this and other similar assertions pushed me into modes of misbehavior. I refused and would not let anyone make or conform me into being similar to, or in any way force me into compliance with, any of my sisters or brothers. I was going to be myself. I was Billy, and I was going to be Billy.

I enjoyed my school life and looked forward to every day of adventuresome activities. I was truly a talkative child and usually sat next to my best friend of that school year, which did not help. In growing up, I had a "best friend" for every year of school. I had other friends, but there was one that just he and I "hung out" at school and talked to on the phone at night. It was generally with this friend that I got in trouble for talking too much. I have report cards that all recorded good grades academically but poor scores in deportment. My report card in the "Teacher's Comments" usually would declare, "Billy is a good student, but he talks a lot." These remarks got me into a lot of trouble at home and earned some corporal disciplines (whippings), but I still talked. I will never forget overhearing a teacher say to another teacher about me, "I think he acts and talks out because he is bored." I did not comprehend her comments then, but later learned she had tried to get me a double promotion, suggesting the advancement would make me have to study harder. Even though the teacher recommended the double promotion, I learned years later that it was actually my mother who was against the advancement. When I asked my mother why she was against the idea, she stated that she wanted me to be with children of my own age.

I must confess that I was a handful in conducting myself in the classroom setting. In fact, I went from being proclaimed and projected by my peers as the eventual class valedictorian to the condescending rank of "class clown." I am guilty of causing a lot of commotion and disquiet in and out of the classroom. I cannot deny or change these facts of life, and now, as an adult, it is not a factum I take pride in.

Years later, at one of our Annie Agnes Wilson High School Alumni Reunions, my classmates did a bit of reminiscing. The conversation eventually evolved to some of the antics that had been instigated by my suggestions and/or where I was the catalyst of these incidents.

When my class comrades would conduct an open forum on my school tactics, many things were told and said of which I honestly have no recollection whatsoever. After listening to the bratty look back of those times, I can truthfully affirm that some of the things that were sounded were factual. However, on the other hand, much of the composition was figments of their imaginations. It was mere fiction, and I didn't remember any of it ever taking place. After listening to their anecdotes, I told them and Tina (my wife) my conclusions on the matter. I told them, "After hearing all the stuff you guys have fabricated against me, it makes me wonder if all they said about Billy the Kid and Jesse James was true!"

Now, I will confess to some (or maybe a lot) of the mischief, but I also know that a lot of the stories were embellished by my classmates. My sister, Dorothy, was present for the "Class Memory Sessions." After hearing the disdainful claims made by my friends, Dorothy stated to Tina and me, "Boy, if Mama and Daddy had known you did all that stuff, you wouldn't be around today!" And she probably was right—thank God for His amazing grace and mercy!

2
GETTING STARTED

I was born into a unique position for favor, at least on one side of my family. On the maternal side of my ancestral family tree, I was just one of the many children born in the same year to the brothers and sisters of my mother. But, on my father's side, I was perfectly aligned by birth to be adored and placed by fate for being adulated and venerated with extraordinary favor of my uncles and aunts.

My father's siblings did not have as many children as those on my mother's side. My father's brothers and sisters were done with childbearing before I was born and, incidentally, there was not a single child born in the year 1948. Therefore, being the "baby" of the family on the paternal side of my family, I was treated like royalty. Everything I did, for the most part, was cute and laughable. I loved it when I was with my dad's side of the family because I knew who would get the brunt of the attention, while on Mom's side, I was "just one of the kids."

I was especially delighted to go on visits to my aunt who lived in Little Rock. My grandmother also lived with my aunt, to add pleasure to the visit. One of the most memorable times involves my aunt's neighbor. The neighbor owned a red, rusted Ford pickup truck. One day, as I looked at the truck out the window, I said, "Look at that old piece-ty truck!" Well, the beauty of this story lies in the fact that my aunt's neighbor had false teeth. I had never seen a set of dentures, and when the neighbor got a particle of food between his gum and teeth, he removed the dentures to give relief to his mouth. Witnessing this new phenomenon, I let out a deathly scream and ran away from the man. It was then explained to me the concept of dentures, but it did not take away my fear of them. The neighbor, from that time on, would use his teeth to playfully (although, not for me) manipulate me into doing whatever he wanted me to do.

Upon hearing my assessment of his truck, my family told the man what I had said. The man told me to come to him, and even though I turned to go the opposite direction, I had to come to him for two reasons: The first reason being that my parents taught me to always respect and obey the elderly. The second reason, and probably more formidably, was that the old man threatened to take out his teeth.

The man sat me on his leg and asked what I had said about his truck. Without missing a beat I immediately blurted out, "I said that you have a *pur-ty* truck!" My quick wit and the ability to lie caused the adults to laugh in an unrestrained fashion; they laughed on and on for some time. This incident that put me in the spotlight felt good and became the substance of jolly times for other visits to Little Rock and the home of my aunt and grandmother.

I tell of this incident to share the special treatment I received on my father's side of the family. This uniqueness was so special that seven years later, when my sister and first cousin gave birth to my nephew and cousin, I detested both with a passion. I had always been the main attraction at my family gatherings, and all of a sudden it was gone, just like that! Two snotty-nosed, unwanted creatures (at least, to me) had come on the scene and claimed the attention that rightfully belonged to me, and I didn't like it at all! No longer was I the star in the meeting of the Blackmons. My jokes and witty remarks did not have the same flare they used to before these unwanted aliens invaded my world, Now, it was all about these two uninvited intruders. They were receiving the attention that belonged to me—it was my entitlement, and for them to have claim to it just wasn't right!

Now, I have to tell you I didn't take all this lying down! I made the lives of these two innocent beings a living hell. I was jealous and loathed them to the highest degree. I won't go into the details of the mistreatments I imposed on my nephew and cousin, only to say it wasn't good. Lest any bring down judgment, I want all to know I have since asked them to forgive me, and feel that they did.

I share this information about growing up to show that much of my personality was developed by activities of my life. I became the one who said something that made people laugh and be happy. It was a good feeling.

When I entered high school, the only thing that marred my home training was my desire to talk when I should have been quiet. I had also become a jokester and learned how to amuse with my jokes and stories. When my mother got wind of my being a humorist and confronted me about it, I informed her that it was all because of her that I liked to see smiles on people's faces.

When I was the only child at home during school hours, I was left home alone with my mother. We were a poor family and my mother had to work to help support the family. My mother did domestic housework in the homes of wealthy people in Malvern ("God's Country") and was allowed to bring me with her as she cleaned their houses. After a long day walking from house to house, my mother was worn to a frazzle from her labor. One sunny day, as we were en route home, I said something (I don't remember what it was) that made my mother laugh out loud. When I looked up at her face, there seemed to be an aura and radiance about her head that has never escaped my memory. That laughter and the smile on my mama's face from that day forward made me feel responsible for keeping my mother laughing when we walked home.

Consequently, when I reached high school, I had learned to command the attention of my class by joking, talking about others, and telling stories, so yes, maybe (a little bit, lightly) I had become the class clown. I loved to have good grades and make the Honor Roll. I took pride in the glory of seeing my name and grades in print for all to see. However, good grades became mitigated to fair grades as I progressed into successive scholastic years. I don't put this part of my life in print out of arrogance, but shame. I developed a practice of staying out with my friends and cared less what my grades looked like. There were also some other habits, and perhaps, when I look back on everything, these other additions may have attributed to my scholarly plummet. But being out and being with my friends was of utmost delight to me. I also realized I was enjoying liberties my older siblings never had.

Now, concerning my gambling habit, it all started when I was in the eighth grade. A first cousin had moved to Malvern ("God's Country") after having gained employment at a local sawmill. This cousin introduced me to the artistry and craftsmanship of throwing dice in the methodical and precise accuracy that assured a win. I learned how to manipulate the dice to make them follow my command. I became pretty good at the art—no brag, just fact! When my parents and sister, Betty (she and I being the only two at home), were asleep, I would take a folded blanket or quilt and practice throwing the dice until the early hours of the morning. Again, a time of my life when had my parents known or caught me, I doubt anyone would be reading this narrative today.

As the adage goes, practice makes perfect. I actually became quite masterful in replicating what I needed for a win. I never had an after-school job, but was able to keep pocket change via my newly acquired skill. I carried this expertise with me through college and onward into my married life. Being from a poor family, I was not blessed with a constant cash flow, so I used my dice-throwing skills to finance my other acquired habits of smoking and drinking. While in college, I was also taught two foolproof card tricks that assured a win every time. These mastered accomplishments allowed me to supplement my financial needs. I was blessed to receive a very small stipend from my father's disability settlement, however, dice were my main source of income at that time. Again, at the risk of sounding a bit conceited, I was a pretty good "small-time" dice shooter. In fact, even now when a certain "homeboy" sees me, he refers to me as "Hard Eight." He contends that if I threw out an eight, I might as well pick up the money, because it as good as made.

I gained respect and built a camaraderie with the neighborhood teens while I attended college. This was a must because of the ominous environment I was living in. Eight of us from Malvern ("God's Country") found housing in a barracks-type apartment building that definitely would not have been my choice of locale had I been able to do better. According to the old saying, however, a man has to do what a man has to do!

The rental property was encompassed from all directions by ruffians who made us know they were in control. We were immediately made aware that we were just occupants in their neighborhood. We learned we were in their world, and they were just letting us live in it!

We were not treated too neighborly by our "neighbors" at first. I don't remember when or how we came into their good graces, but we did. To the best of my recollection, I think it began when I walked up on them under a streetlight where four or five of the "little darlings" were shooting dice on the sidewalk. I had previously become acquainted with and somewhat befriended two of the teens who vouched on my behalf as "being all right." I was allowed to participate in their game of chance. I was careful not to win, since there wasn't much money to be had, and also not to risk offending my newly formed friends.

From that night forward I had guardian angels watching over me. Yes, it was like the old Black negro hymn, "All day, all night, the angels are watching over me." The high schoolers eventually began coming to my room, as they said, to "take your money." I will never forget one of the youngsters telling the others, "Y'all, old Billy ain't nothing but an old dice slickster." I quickly denied the claim and was the first to laugh it off.

Looking back over those years, I can see God's hand of protection, even though I was unaware of it. I shall never forget one gambling event I took part in. I don't remember how I found out about the game, but it was a neighborhood man that I rode with to the house of the event. I was in a section of the city I had never been in, in the company of people (teens and adults) I didn't know. I was somewhat fearful at first, but was made to feel comfortable by their cordiality and friendliness.

I didn't have much money that night, but I didn't need much; the night belonged to me. Every throw of the dice was mine. Whatever I threw out, I made the point. I made everything! I was clicking on all eight cylinders—I was on, I was a winner! Whatever I did was the right thing to do, it all worked to my favor. The throw-out number, the amount I was shooting for, the side bets—I was raking it in! I didn't take the time to count my winnings while I was in action because, as the songwriter says, "You don't count your money at the table, there's plenty time to do that when the game is done." However, if I was to guesstimate, I would say I had fifteen hundred to two thousand dollars in my hand at one time.

Then, it happened. At about one a.m. my luck began to go south. I literally went from good to bad quickly. Nothing I did or threw was a winner, and even my dice manipulation failed me. Everything I did or tried to do was unsuccessful. The big winner was fast becoming the big loser. Seeing my luck changing, I was wise and cunning enough to slide two one-hundred-dollar bills into my socks without being detected by the other gamblers.

After declaring my losses, I left the house and paid a man to take me home since my ride had gone a few hours earlier. The driver and I lamented my rotten luck as we discussed the fallacy of depending on "Lady Luck." I was disgusted, to say the least, that I came away a loser, but next day grapevine news made me grateful. I was told the eventful winner was found later lying on the ground outside the gambling house. The big winner had been knocked in the head and robbed. Except, by the grace of God, there lay I!

This incident would have made a wiser man walk away and abandon such a habit. It did help me in a single way. I vowed to myself never to gamble in places I'm not acquainted with or with people I don't know. I now realize, but for the grace of God, the face on the ground found assaulted that morning could very well have been mine. Thank You, dear God, for keeping me even when I'm not aware of Your presence and protection.

The memory of that night and what could have happened stayed with me for a while, but having no job, "need more" was on my back. There were also this insatiable and constant want to buy and get things that had a grip on me. I resorted to what opened doors for me and what I did best. I went back to the dice games to do what I had to do. However, I went back with a new mindset and some personal rules and promises. I vowed never to gamble with people I don't know or in unfamiliar places. I amended these to only gamble in day hours and be gone by sundown. Greed and available money washed up that claim pretty quickly to make that declaration altogether null and void.

3
HABITS

As I stated in chapter one, to me, my parents lived humdrum lives and did not do any "cool" stuff. They didn't use colorful profanity, they didn't smoke, and they didn't drink. My parents were just a couple of uncool "fuddy-duddies" and didn't know how to have fun. They were anemic and lusterless in the enjoyments of life. How could they do this to me? I mean, after all, since they weren't rich, at the least they should have known how to have some less mundane qualities and appreciations for life.

Growing up, I was thankful for intriguing grownup neighbors who, in my opinion, knew how to have fun. I admired and emulated adults outside of my home as I watched them indulge in the masterful art of non–Sunday School words of profanity and behaviors like blowing smoke out their nostrils after lighting a cigarette. I'd visit another home and witness the iced frosted glasses filled with sudsy beer or some other alcohol beverage. Now, these folks knew how to have fun. Why hadn't my parents attended the "how to enjoy life" school?

Then, one day, I came home and to my utter amazement, there in the kitchen, in the metallic cabinet, was a six-pack of Pabst Blue Ribbon beer. I thought I had entered the Twilight Zone, or at the least, I had entered the wrong house. My mind was racing with thoughts of hilarious mental notions. My parents had finally arrived! Mama and Daddy, or at least one of them, had come over to the caliber of parent I had desired for so long. However, my merriment was short-lived and immediately dashed when my father explained the reason for the beer being in the house. It seemed Daddy had contracted some kind of urinary tract infection and the doctor had prescribed the beer to clear up the problem by flushing out his kidneys. Drats! What a letdown, and I wasn't even able to steal a single can.

Admiration for our neighbors and their habits drew me near to next-door homes that I frequented as much as my own. I thoroughly enjoyed the felicity and bonds I had contrived with my elderly neighbors. I was with them as often and for as long as I possibly could be. There was one friendship I especially treasured. When no one was around, this grand old man would actually let me taste his beer. Just a sip, but boy, was it good! There I was, no one would believe it! I was actually drinking beer! Oh, the taste of those bubbly and tasteful suds! It was love at first taste!

I started to spend more time with this neighbor and was able to get my watery taste buds satisfied. Man, was that stuff good! The more I was given, the more I craved. Now, my neighbor also consumed stronger intoxicants, and even let me sip a taste of the hard stuff. However, the more potent liquors did not appeal to me at all. They burned my mouth and scorched my innards as they went down, singeing my internal organs. He could keep the hard liquors—just give me the beer.

That was the beginning of my love for the barley and hops concoction. My friendship with this special adult friend was marred by my parents eventually curtailing my visits to his home. They did not stop my visits to his home totally, but forcefully and verbally suggested I spend less time over there. I don't know what transpired within the adult world. All I know is that my fraternity with this grown man was diminished and ultimately came to an abrupt end. When I look back on that era of my life, I have concluded that it was a corporate and mutual decision arrived at by the general consensus of "old folk."

There I was, enjoying life to the fullest, growing up and innocently learning to appreciate the "finer things" in life. Then, all of a sudden, I had the rug pulled out from under my feet. It was engineered and orchestrated by a commanding parental insistence against my visiting and "hanging out" with this older man. But what could be the problem? After all, he was respected in the community and a citizen of respectable means. So, why were my parents hassling me over visiting this dear neighbor? And then, to make matters worse, the man himself seemed to have turned against me. He didn't appear as hospitable as he had been in the past. The worst possible castigation of this period of my young life that could ever happen was coming to pass. My neighbor quit being my friend and bartender; he no longer gave me beer.

The damage, however, had been done. I had been exposed, I had been caught up—I had developed a taste and love for beer. As a preteen, I wanted to satisfy my predilection for the savory brew, but was unable to get it. After all, I lived in a dry county (although alcohol was being "bootlegged") and was unable to purchase alcohol since I was underage, and also did not have the financial resources to make the purchase.

I had to wait until I was old enough and could pay for

the gratification of my liquid appetite. Beer was only fifty cents a can by the time I reached my teenage years. When I was in high school, I was able to buy my first car for five dollars and a dog. The car was a 1950 Chevrolet four-door coupe. For five dollars, even then, you can imagine I did not have much of a car. I had a little knowledge of auto mechanics, and with the help of my father (who did most of the work), I was able to have my own car in high school.

So now, with transportation, I was on the move about town. I knew the bootleggers (those who sold liquor illegally), especially a woman who had known my family and me for years. I was able to drive to this particular house, make a purchase, and leave with none the wiser. How cool was that, huh?

It was at that conjecture of my life that I learned through experience both the need and importance of having enough money to enjoy a desirable lifestyle. I had a car, I was now able to buy beer, and I was even the envy of some of my peers because I had a car. However, the real truth of the matter is that with life comes responsibilities that also bring a price tag. I had a car that required gas, oil, tires, and maintenance. I never had insurance on the vehicle and don't even know if insurance was lawfully required at this time. I had no job, but I had responsibilities and needs that only money could answer.

Having no job brought me no great concern at the time since I was able to satisfy my money needs by engaging in the dice game of chance. I would instigate a gathering at school that would result in dice shooting. We would go to the boy's restroom (with someone on the lookout for administration) for this business. We also had certain homes that were nearby where both parents worked and made these our gambling dens. These homes were ideal for us since they were so close to the school that we would only be gone for a short time. It meant skipping a few classes, but we were, in a sense, being exposed to mathematics (I'm being sarcastic). These games helped me in managing to keep gas money and a little pocket change to finance the other costs of my lifestyle.

By this time, I had picked up a habit that I had vehemently sworn I would never take up. This decision was spontaneous from an earlier experience of my childhood that marred my desire for tobacco. This resolution was via an accursed event that, even now, when I think about it, sickens me. When I was about ten or eleven years old, I came about (better yet, I stole) a Savana Sweet cigar from a ma-and-pa store. Selfless by nature (and scared to be alone), I shared my fortune with a friend. We got some matches and made our trek into some nearby woods. Puffing like two locomotive trains, we savored the coarse burn of the fiery effects of the fumigated tobacco rolls.

Huffing and puffing on the cigar was an exhilarating encounter. It was quite manly and delightful as we blew smoke into the air. As long as we just puffed and blew the smoke into the air, everything went all right. The problem came about when we decided to do it right by inhaling the vapors. Round and round, like a spinning roulette, the earth took orbit. We both became so queasy that we found ourselves profusely throwing up.

We lay on the ground and stayed in the woods until we were physically able and energized (mentally and strength-wise) to navigate ourselves home. When I got home, all I could do was toss and turn as my world accelerated uncontrollably in orbit through our solar system. Of course, I would, by necessity, have to get up to relieve myself from nausea with a healthy round of upchucking.

Even now, after the passing of many years, I still recall the agonizing and horrific feeling of that day. I made myself on that selfsame day a personal vow to never smoke again.

When I muse over the occurrences of my growing-up days, particularly that of smoking, it still affects me mentally. There is another happening I remember that should have discouraged me from picking up the tobacco habit. When I was in the seventh or eighth grade, I had a gruesome and repulsive encounter. I write the following statement not as a complaint, for God has been extremely good to me. I was born into a poverty-stricken family with limited utilities in our home. It was years before our home had the blessings of an indoor lavatory.

Having shared that bit of information, I will go on with my story. I had started to smoke by now, and in the ninth or tenth grade, my choice of smoking brand was a cigarette called Tareyton. The Tareyton had a specialized filter that was boasted to contain charcoal to give the product a better taste. My brand had a coined slogan, "Us Tareyton smokers would rather fight than switch!" By now I had fully developed the smoking habit and had the "nicotine monkey" on my back. I was hooked, and the addiction had me. However, as I earlier indicated, my mother and father did not smoke and taught their children against the usage of tobacco products (I now know I had some smart parents). Therefore, out of respect and fear (probably the greater reason) for my parents, I smoked in secret.

Late at night, when I felt that everyone was asleep, I would slip out of the house to the "toilet" or "outhouse" for a smoke to satisfy my nicotine addiction. On this particular evening I got my smokes (cigarettes) and matches out of my hiding place and made my way to the toilet. I struck the match and lit my cigarettes like I had done many times before. However, tonight's experience was different. This cigarette did not taste like my beloved brand. This cigarette was the worst blend I had ever tasted. I nevertheless kept puffing while thinking that whatever was causing that gosh-awful taste would burn away and allow me to enjoy the real taste.

It was not to be, though. The longer I puffed in that fiery incinerate, the more disgusting the taste became. It got to the point that not only did it taste bad, but it started to be hard to pull in the smoke. I kept puffing and inhaling, then all of a sudden there was a burning sensation in my throat. I became fearful because of the pain and immediately extinguished the cigarette. There was too much left to throw away, so I put the remainder back into the pack.

I sneaked back into the house and climbed back into bed. It was a miserable and long, long night. Fear intensified in my mind as I wondered what was happening to me. My throat was burning, throbbing, and felt as if it were collapsing in. I was terrified, to say the least, but I couldn't tell my parents because they would kill me (what an irony). In my reasoning, it was better to take my chances on my throat opening up than to face the wrath of two angry anti-smoking parents.

Needless to say, it was a long, rigid, and fearful night. I didn't know if I would see the morning light. I slept very little, if any, on that hideous night. But, by the grace of God, I made it and was able to witness the dawning of a new day. My throat was inflamed, my mouth was dry, and the fear of death petrified my thoughts. It was indeed a scary time!

When the morning light finally chased the darkness away and I was able to see, I checked out my cigarette stash. I was astonished when I saw what I had done. In the darkness of the night, I had mistakenly lit the charcoal end of the cigarette. The charcoal end of the filter had charred, bringing on a toxic effect that had irritated my throat and air passage. It bothered me to swallow, and even spittle going down caused a sizzle of pain at every ingestion. The pain lasted for nearly two weeks.

Now, you would think that after these two traumatic experiences I would have nothing to do with smoking and tobacco. But, oh no, not the case with me. I liked smoking—it was a cool thing to do. Also, by this time, I was addicted to cigarettes and could not free myself from the habit.

Let me share how I came about becoming a smoker. Even though my childhood cigar and botched smoking episodes should have hampered my partaking of tobacco goods, I got caught up and consequently became addicted. Yes, I was taught against smoking and had vowed never to smoke, but I abandoned all my convictions. I literally hung around people who smoked. I simply hung around the wrong crowd. I came about smoking via association with the folk I ran with—they smoked, and I ended up smoking!

I didn't realize it at that time, but there is in the Word of God a warning against what happens when you partner with the wrong company. The King James Version of the Bible in 1 Corinthians 15:33 states, "Be not deceived: evil communication corrupts good manners." The Interlinear Hebrew-Greek-English Bible quotes the verse to say, "Do not be led astray: bad companionship ruins good habits."

Then, again, in 1 Corinthians 5:6b (KJV) asks the question, "Don't you know that a little leaven leaventh the whole loaf?" The New International Version interprets the same verse as, "Don't you know that a little yeast works through the whole batch of dough?"

Bad communication ruined me, and when I started, I

could not see how a little cigarette could be so bad. After all, I was in control of my body and could quit whenever I wanted to. I was successful for quite some time, as I would smoke for a while and quit when I chose to. However, the day came where the old saying "If you play with fire, you will get burnt" became woefully true. The day came when I was burnt and could not lay the "cancer sticks" down. The nicotine habit had abducted me—I was addicted!

I cannot put total blame on anyone else, but by hanging with the wrong company, I was influenced and drawn into some wrong deeds and, perhaps, some unsavory habits. However, let me make this extrication: I am not saying my associates were bad people or that they caused me to take up the habit of smoking. I have never blamed anyone else for my malignant actions; whatever I did, I did it because I wanted to do it. I will not and will never cast blame on another person for my actions. I take full responsibility and accountability for my deportment. After all, I'm sure I introduced many of my peers to some pernicious ways, especially those associated with dice shooting.

So, here I am now, a high school teenager with some expensive possessions and some costly habits. I'm an adolescent who has a car that brought with it liabilities and weighty responsibilities of gas, oil, and upkeep. If that wasn't enough, I had complicated my life with the acquired habit of smoking and an enamored taste for beer.

Since I had no job to depend on for a reliable source of income, I did what I did best. I shot dice. Whenever and wherever I spotted a group of young men gathered together, I would approach them with the hopes and proposition that would lead the crowd to a game of chance—shooting dice. There was never enough money to get rich, but it was enough to get by for that day. It got to the point that my gambling "friends" would exclude me from the game since I usually came out as the big winner (I won what little was to be had). They really made it easier for me by the exclusion; I would find out who the "big winner" was, then simply and conveniently look him up and walk away with the winnings.

I had a few habits that captivated my mind, body, and what little money I had. When I look back on those times, I can see that if I had had the fortitude of resistance, my life would have been a lot less complicated. With that being said, I have tried to use those experiences to a better life for Christ and to warn others of the pitfalls associated with these habits.

4
GOING FORWARD

Time goes on, and with time, so does life. I was now a young man with high and glamorous ambitions. I'd grown older, but my level of maturity left a lot to be desired. I had finished high school, attended college, married, become a father, and become gainfully employed. God blessed me with fairly good jobs to adequately provide for my family.

I was young, and even though I sporadically attended church, I definitely was not living a Christian life. My life was filled with indulging in loose and vile habits. At this point in my life, I was guilty of profanity, drinking, gambling, and infidelity. My life had spun out of control with no end in sight for a change for the better, due much to the fact that I thought I was having fun. However, as time went on, I became disgusted with my activities and life. Eventually, by the grace of God, from the cesspool of a polluted hog pen, I came to myself. I came back to the church and rededicated myself to the Lord. I confessed my sins and rejoined myself to the body of believers in Jesus Christ. I became faithful in attendance, with my family, to my church (First Baptist Church, Vine Street) in Malvern

("God's Country"). I attended Sunday School, Morning and Evening Worship Services, Baptist Training Union, and even became a contemporary of Wednesday Evening Bible Study and Prayer Meetings.

I awakened into spiritual growth and maturity by levels of degrees. I recommitted my life to the Lord and did so from a true and contrite heart. I meant what I said and had every intention of putting forth real and zealous effort to be the man God wanted me to be. I wanted to be a great light for Jesus and to love Him with all my heart, mind, soul, and strength. However, in keeping with the integrity of truth, I was unable to maintain it in my life initially. I was more than able to identify with Apostle Paul's declaration in Romans 7:15 (KJV), "For that which I do I allow not: for what I would, that I do not; but what I hated, that I do." Amen! Amen!

I wanted then, as I do now, to live a life totally committed to the Lordship of Jesus Christ. I wanted to, I strove to, I desired to live a life emancipated and empowered by the Holy Spirit. I knew I had been washed by the blood of Jesus Christ and craved to live an existence worthy of His Holy Name as a Christian. I found comfort in and thank God that He allowed Paul, under the influence of the Holy Spirit, to write in Romans 7:18 (KJV), "For I know that in me [that is, in my flesh], there dwelleth no good thing: for to will is present with me: but how to perform that which is good I find not. For the good that I would I do not: but the evil that I would not, that I do. Now, if I do that I would not, it is no more that I do it, but sin that dwelleth in me. I find then a law, that when I would do good, evil is present with me."

Even in my detestable condition and situation, I was encouraged to know that the stalwart and epitome character of Christianity, Apostle Paul, related to a sinner like me. This great man of faith strengthened me with a testimony common to all of the human race. It helped me to know that one of the greatest characters in the Bible expressed my fleshly fallacies as well. Praise God for the man of God and his sharing of his struggles in the Christian warfare.

Now that I had learned I was not alone and isolated in the subterfuge and deception of Satan and the flesh, I found an inner power and consolation. I knew I was real in my desire and quest to live a Godly and righteous life to the honor and glory of God through His Son, Jesus Christ. All that was within me, with all my physical, psychic, and spiritual being, I wanted to live to the fullest, a life pledged to the Lord.

But alas, the complications emancipated from inward, insatiable desires driven by the lust of the eyes and flesh. My mind was constantly bombarded with illicit and lewd temptations. The enticements were great, and I found myself rising and falling to sinful seductions. I didn't want to live this way, but I just couldn't seem to help myself. I truly wanted to live a life that would witness to the power of God; I genuinely desired to let my light so shine that men might see my good works and also glorify my Father in heaven. However, the truth of the matter was that I truly did not like me and what I had become.

I grew weary in trying to live a Godly and pure life. The more I attempted to subsist on a righteous life, seemingly the stronger the temptation would be. Satan hoodwinked and beguiled me with hypocrisy and the falsified excuse that nobody is perfect and that we all sin. With this false sense of security, I was pacified and soothed with excuses for my ungodly lifestyle. Satan even comforted me through misinterpretation of the Scriptures. The Deceiver convinced me that Romans 3:3 (KJV) covered my situation when Paul wrote, "All have sinned and come short of the glory of God." He then wrapped my mind in a security blanket to think God understood my weaknesses. That rascal deluded me into making me interpret this verse as plausibility for excusing my promiscuous and evil ways. Yes, it is true that all have sinned and all have fallen short of His glory. That fact alone tells the world that God knows we are all sinners and made it possible for an escape through His Son, Jesus Christ—it's all there in His Word!

I am so grateful and thank God that also contained in His Word is the power of the Holy Spirit. He gives the enthusiasm and might of truth for inspiration and Godly living. Even though Satan has used the Scriptures for deception, God convicted me in the truth of His Word. Yes, I had sinned and truly fallen short of the glory of God—all so true! The Devil had successfully diluted the Word of God to make me secure in sin.

The Master Trickster made me feel comfortable in the fact that I am a part of the depraved human race and inclusive of that truth. I'm so appreciative that God's Holy Spirit would not allow me to rest in that impious interpretation. The Lord led me to 1 John 1:8 and 9 (KJV), "If we say we have no sin, we deceive ourselves, and the truth is not in us. If we confess our sins, He is faithful and just to forgive us our sins, and to cleanse us from all unrighteousness." Then, it is further written in 2 Peter 3:9 (KJV), "The Lord is not slack concerning His promise; but is longsuffering to usward, not willing that any should perish, but that all should come to repentance."

These verses gave me a new concept of thought and understanding. Yes, Satan, I have sinned, I am guilty, I am a part of and can join the anthropomorphic chorus of all humanity; I have sinned and come short of the glory of God—AGAIN! I admit it, I confess it from my heart, I agree with God that I have sinned!

Woe is me! What shall I do, O wretched man that I am! Who shall deliver me from the body of this death? What a lamentable situation I find myself in. Oh, what a distressing predicament I am accosted and confronted with. How did I become enslaved and captured by that which I hate and despise? And then, a more prevalent question that I should be asking myself is, "How can I get out of the mess I have gotten myself in?"

When I was almost ready to give up, ready to throw in the towel, a spiritual lifeline was thrown out to me. God's Holy Spirit renewed my faith and hope as He guided me to the answer. In Romans 7:24 and 25 (KJV), it is written, "O wretched man that I am! Who shall deliver me from the body of this death? I thank God through Jesus Christ our Lord. So then, with my mind I myself serve the law of God, but with the flesh the law of sin."

The law of sin overpowered me to the satisfaction of the weaknesses of my mind and flesh. My sin(s) are ever before me; how could I allow myself to come here again? Oh wretched man that I am! Who shall deliver me from this terrible situation? What shall I do? Who can I call on for immediate help? I need help and I need it now! Somebody, please! I need help instantly, right now! My dilemma is more than I can handle.

I was at my lowest when, in my spirit, I seemed to hear the Lord say, "What did I say in My Word?" It was then that He reminded me that if I confess, if I say the same thing about my sin as God says, I can be saved. When I did, I could actually feel a sense of cleansing in my mind and spirit. God is real, He is faithful, and anyone who comes to

Him with a true and contrite heart will be forgiven of her/his sins. Praise God for His amazing grace and pardoning love!

We ought all be grateful to a Heavenly Father Who loves us so much that when we come to Him in repentance, admitting and confessing our sins, He will forgive us. God truly loves us and doesn't want anyone to die in their sins and be condemned to a place of eternal damnation and everlasting destruction.

Even though we are all sinners and have sinned, we must continue going forward in the Lord God. The King James Version expresses it best toward humanity in the beloved John 3:16, "For God so loved the world that He gave His Only Begotten Son, that whosoever believeth in Him should not perish, but have everlasting life." It is there in His Word! In going forward, the best start is the Bible—all a person needs is in His Word!

5
THE STRUGGLE

Years of spiritual struggling, ups and downs, joys and tears, times of jubilation, and times of depression went by. There was very little change in my life as I engaged in spiritual warfare with the wiles of the Devil and the lust of my flesh. It was a daily internal fight of both spiritual and physical combat. The only real noticeable difference in my life was that I was now a regular and faithful member of my church, First Baptist, Vine Street.

Days and weeks went by with the same repeated actions. I lived a life of duplicity, living two opposing lifestyles. Six days a week were satiated with ungodly living, and then I would feel cleansed by attending God's place of worship on Sunday. I didn't like myself nor my deeds. I wanted to live a life of purity and holiness. I deeply desired to live for the Lord, but the truth of the matter was that I was failing Him miserably and had become no more than a religious hypocrite.

An average week of my life consisted of going to work, then coming home to gulp down a family meal, if you could call it that. It was my family's rule that we eat one meal together every day as a unit. And so I had to eat with my family to set my established standard. I would then rush out of the house to be with "the boys." We would meet at the home of an older man in his enclosed garage to play dominoes. The evening composition of my sinful life was alcohol (beer), smoking, profanity, lying, gambling, and being around drugs. I did not partake in drugs, but I think the odor in the air did something to me. Overall, in my mind, it was a time to relax and unwind from a hard day's work ("stinking thinking" from the Devil).

However, when Friday came, there was a change of venue that carried me to a different locale. The scene would change from an enclosed garage to the smoke-filled "clubs" or "juke joints" on the outskirts of town. Although it was a "dry county" (so called because liquor was not sold) and gambling was illegal, there were many clubs, liquor houses, and places of gambling. It was always rumored that the local sheriff was receiving a payoff to look the other way on the unlawful activities. I frequented two of those illegal establishments each Friday and Saturday evening/morning to satisfy my vice and love for gambling.

My big quest was to win a big jackpot, dump it into my wife's lap, and then retire from gambling. After all, I was a pretty good small-town "dice shooter." I usually won, but the winnings were never enough to let me retire. Dice was my greatest corruption. When I look back over those times, although I didn't realize it then, it was clear I had a gambling addiction. I arrived at that conclusion from the fact that it did not matter whether I won or lost—I just loved to hear the clattering of those dice in my hands! There's got to be something wrong with a person's psyche when that person doesn't care or mind parting from his or her hard-earned money with nothing in return. It was worsened by the fact that there was no remorse, only satisfaction to hear those rattling cubes.

After years of this merry-go-round cycle of living, I began to have a dislike for myself and what I had become. I literally despised myself for letting my life get to this state of existence. I was a churchgoing pretender. Then, to make matters worse, there came a period that each Sunday the preacher's messages seemed to be targeting me. It became so beseeming that the pastor was "picking" on me that I accused my wife of telling him what I was doing.

Unaware of what Satan was doing, I followed his subliminal insinuations and stopped going to church. No sir! I would not have it and didn't have to put up with that. That preacher had enough other sins that he could preach about and harp on without lecturing on my faults every Sunday. I didn't mind him preaching to me sometimes, but wasn't he supposed to preach to everybody? Why was he just meddling with me? Well I'll show him, I won't tolerate it! I just won't come to church so regularly.

I followed my threat to a tee. I curtailed and abridged my churchgoing attendance tremendously. It got to the point that I would describe and consign myself to what I call "Special Day" membership. I was part of that elite group who only show up to church on Easter, Mother's Day, and Christian holidays. The pathetic part of my bad decision and habit was that the longer I stayed away, the less my not going bothered me.

Although my absenteeism, at times, tormented me, the Devil brought a soothing consolation to my mind. Satan allowed me to live with my conscience through watching the lives of others. After all, many of the people in these hangouts with me were confessed Christians (maybe I should refer to them as "church members") who would be in church tomorrow morning. What a shame! What a disgrace! Those hypocrites! Out here with me on Saturday night and tomorrow morning, up in the church! At least I'm not like them, I'm keeping it real! I really felt good in comparing myself and knowing I was not like them. I was not sitting up in the church and being a hypocrite. (Boy, was I nervy!)

The people I criticized and held disdain toward had no knowledge of my accusations against them unless someone in my circle told them. What entitlement could I possibly have to put anyone down? I have no answer and cannot, even to this day, justify those remarks of ill critique. Even though they were not living perfect lives, they were a lot better off than I was by a long shot. They were, after all, going to a place where they could get help. They were sick people (like me) who were going to the spiritual hospital. Nobody would denigrate a person for going to a doctor or hospital seeking help for their infirmities. They may have to return frequently to the place where healing can be procured if the cure is not immediately achieved. Jesus declares in Mathew 9:9 (KJV), "They that be whole need not a physician but they that are sick." These sick folk, unlike me, were at least at the right place where they could get help. God be thanked for His infinite wisdom and the establishing of His Church in bringing healing to the hearts and minds of men, women, boys, and girls all over the world.

There I was, hating myself and who I had become, while at the same time loving and enjoying what I was doing. My life was not what I desired it to be—I was trapped! My routine weekly activities consisted of work, dominoes, dice, cigarettes, beer, and other unmentionables that I don't care to list at this time. Depressed and disgusted with myself, I would at times cry out to God in prayer for deliverance. My prayers were often accompanied by tears of sorrow, however (being totally truthful), there was no real repentance.

I am grateful that since that time I have learned that, according to the Word of God, no forgiveness of sins can be obtained without a heart of repentance. The King James Version quotes Paul writing in 2 Corinthians 7:10, "For godly sorrow worketh repentance to salvation not to be repented of: but the sorrow of the world worketh death." Repentance involves the changing of the mind, and Paul says that when a person is truly sorry for the wrong deeds done in his or her life, salvation is possible.

It is not enough to have mere sorrow, but a regretful mind is also needed in the process of repentance. There is a possibility that a person can repent but their sorrow doesn't work the right kind of repentance. There is a repentance that is not Godly, since a person can repent and only be sorry that she or he got caught. God wants us to confess or agree with Him in righteousness concerning the errors of our ways and then turn to Him for power to sustain a holy and sanctified life. The message of John the Baptist and Jesus Himself, upon breaking on the stage of history, brought the same message: "Repent ye: for the kingdom of heaven is at hand" (Matthew 3:2; 4:17 (KJV)).

I wanted to live a life of purity that would glorify God and bring edification to all I come in contact with. This concept has always been my desired objective, but the accomplishing of it was an entirely different subject. This inward struggle was continuous, and I could not seem to bring it to pass. It seemed I would never be what I wanted to be, much less what God wanted me to be. What a mess I've made of myself!

The affairs of my life were configurations of disappointing setbacks that were taking me in the opposite direction of where I wanted to go. Life had presented a paradox of contradictory consequences and dilemmas. I knew my life was not what I wanted it to be and was definitely not fitting in the eyes of an all-wise, pure, and holy God.

I was in the world where I didn't want to be, doing things I really didn't want to do. The inner struggle was so devastating and overwhelming since, instead of doing better, I seemed to be getting worse. The plaguing accuracy of my deplorable plight was that I knew the Word of God to declare that if a person draws near to God, He will draw near to the person.

Even though, in my mind and heart, I genuinely desired to live a righteous life, the opposite was my reality. Instead of achieving holiness, I had increasingly become viler. I took a candid evaluation of myself and did not like the concluded results and confirmation that faced me. The more I wanted to live a sanctified life, the further I seemed to collapse into a more depraved course of existence.

Here I was, a man who had become overcome with insipid and unwanted habits of personal dislikes. I found myself entangled with vices and sins that were appalling to me. I tried to overcome my transgressions by my own might, but found myself helpless, and to say the least, hopeless. I despised that I had become addicted to cigarettes, a love for beer, and a compulsion for gambling. These habits had captivated me and brought me into their control and dominance. The struggle worsened greatly to victimize me as prey. My human powers and strength were suppressed by the battles within me. Instead of overcoming my faults, my faults got the best of me; in fact, I became worse with time. By now I was not only a smoker, drinker, and gambler, but had also adapted to other disgraceful trespasses. Not only was I confronted with all these sinful infirmities, I became challenged with lying and other unmentionable shortcomings. The struggle was constant and compelling!

One of the quandaries of life that has plagued the human race is the makeup of fleshy composition. A person has the mind to do what is right and good in relation to God and fellow beings. Each person truly has every intention to work to make this world a better place by promoting love, peace, and good will toward all. She or he is determined to carry out the doctrines of good as prescribed by the Lord in His Word. Ready, game, and willing, the person ventures out to create a better environment for the inhabitants of the earth. The person is motivated to be the best that she or he can be for righteousness' sake.

However, dismay and discouragement set in when the person fails to carry out the ideal through transformation and actuality. The words of Apostle Paul ring true: "The things that I would do, I do not and things that I would not are the things that I do. Whenever I wanted to and would do good, evil is present with me that the good that I do, I do not!"

This is where I was. What can I do? Somebody, please give me an escape route; show me, please, the exit door! The struggle is overwhelming, Lord, help me—I need a "fix" to get out of this "fix"! Oh, what a struggle!

6
BACK AGAIN

Life and God have ways of bringing about change, which lead to either good or to bad. One of the things I have learned in my sojourn on the earth is that time is replete with changes. Life is permeated with untimely, and invariably most always, unwanted fluctuations.

Humanity has no options or say-so in the matter at all. I think Job expressed it best in his fitting oral expression in Job 14:1 (KJV): "Man that is born of a woman is of a few days, and full troubles." Then Solomon, in the fullness of his wisdom, seems to "Amen" Job's judgment when he declares in Ecclesiastes 2:23, "For all his (man) days are sorrows, and his travail grief; yea, his heart taketh not rest in the night. This also is vanity."

Life is jam-packed with capricious and unpredictable renovations. A person will, by virtue of being alive, often face and be compelled to maneuver head-on his or her incalculable situations. A person can never remain the same, for life demands change. No one is exempt or free from the experience of emancipation. Change is taxed on all of mankind and must be dealt with physically, mentally, and spiritually.

My time and change materialized gradually, and unforeseen. I took delight in the things I was doing. However, in the unsuspected tense of times and events I experienced discontentment at the same time. It was not calculated or planned on my calendar of happenings for the day. It just hit me with such a devastating force that I had to look at myself and what I had become.

It was during this period of my life that I did not like what I saw or what my personal survey revealed to me about myself. I had not been a good husband, father, or person. I had been blessed by God to be employed by companies that allowed me to afford adequate care for my family. I was able to supply all of our basic needs and also some of the things our hearts desired. We were not rich by any stretch of the imagination, but I was blessed to be able to give my family above-average care. My income was also supplemented by my dice-shooting talents and winnings.

The small city of Malvern ("God's Country") had a population of approximately ten thousand people. The town proudly boasted and gloated in the fact that there was a payday by some business or company every day of the week. The town was blessed to have job employment that paid decent wages. Workers could find a paying assignment at one of the three sawmills, one of the three brickyards (brick manufacturers), Flakeboard Plant (particle board manufacturer), or the aluminum plant. There was also always available work in the "Billet" (short cuts of wood), cutting and hauling.

There was plenty of work for any able-bodied person who wanted to work in and around Malvern ("God's Country"). As with any assessment, there was a perceived estimation and division of financial worthiness. Reynolds Metals Company (an aluminum producer) was by far considered by most to be the supreme local workplace. In fact, it was a known fact around Malvern ("God's Country") that if you worked for Reynolds, anything in the city was available to you. Working for Reynolds was equivalent to being awarded the key to the city. If you worked for Reynolds Metals, instant unlimited credit lines and buying power were automatic gifts.

I was blessed to be hired by Reynolds Metals Company and was granted a speed induction into the "chosen few" for absolute buying power. I ended up at the Reynolds Metals plant about forty miles from Malvern ("God's Country"), but it did not matter, it was Reynolds. I bring out all this to testify of the goodness and grace of God toward me. It was God's blessing that I was able to give my family a comfortable life. God was extremely favorable to me in supplying above adequacy for the Blackmon household needs (and some wants also).

Life was good! I had landed a well-paying job, was blessed with a healthy family, my marriage was intact—I was living large! We were indeed blessed to be able to build a new house and to buy our first new car. I was able to purchase whatever we needed and a lot of what we just wanted. These things were accomplished on one source of income. This was a special blessing to assure the reality and fertility of my prayers. I had always wanted that my wife would be able to stay home with our children. God did it for me, and I can testify to all that He will give us the desires of our hearts.

The only problem with being able to buy is that you also have to pay for your purchases. I bought and was buying, but unfortunately, I discounted the fact that I was accountable for those costs. I had no budget and disregarded the wisdom of my wife, who warned me betimes. Because of my business incompetence, I brought on myself and my household a weighty financial burden. My buying power activated a troublesome time in my life and the Blackmon ménage.

Life had changed and my world was crumbling down around me. I was heavily indebted and saw no way out of my deplorable situation. I was now beholden to a burden too heavy for me to bear. My finances were not the only complications I was confronted with. I also had my habits and weekend activities that had to be financed. I was worried and depression invaded my thoughts constantly. My world was closing in on me and I had not the least inkling as to how to conquer my dismal and disconsolate quandary.

Financial obligation, coupled with my habits, had gotten the best of me and were taking a toll mentally. All of a sudden, my life seemed to be spiraling in a downward revolution. The problems were mounting up and were very real. They were so vastly manifested that there was no way they could be overlooked. I had a good job that paid great wages and I was doing pretty good at the tables of chance with the dice. All of this was working in my favor, but it was never enough—I was in a dilemma! My bills were becoming greater than my income, and I just didn't seem to have sufficient funds to cover all that was demanded of me.

I began to succumb to my problems mentally and physically. Worry and distress captivated my every waking thought. I wasn't able to sleep, and my appetite decreased tremendously. I didn't know what to do, but being a man who had to be in charge, I knew I had to do something. Being in charge was a high priority with me, therefore it was a matter I had to subdue. What to do was beyond me, but I knew I had to get the situation under control.

Looking back over those lean years, I can see an increase

of engagements in my smoking, drinking, gambling, and loose behavior. The behavior in the increased purchases of these items added to my spending woes, and God knows I certainly did not need that since I could not afford it.

There was little change in my daily and weekly schedule of activities. My normal day remained: going to work, coming home, gulping down a meal at the family table, and then rushing off to play dominoes with "the boys." When the weekend rolled around, beginning with Friday evening through Saturday night I could be found at one of the two local clubs trying to get rich shooting dice.

I was going through some hard times, but I was young and had a brash confidence in myself with thoughts that elevated me above other men and my circumstances. I honestly felt I could hold my own with any man. The truth of the matter is that I didn't think anyone could whip me in a one-on-one hand-to-hand confrontation. I also felt there was no situation or circumstance that may arise that I couldn't eventually overcome. Some may call my attitude of positivism cockiness, but nevertheless, this was my mindset.

As time progressed and I continued to carry on the same lifestyle, I began to tire of it all. My life and successes were nothing like I had projected for myself and hoped for them to be. I was heavily in debt, a bad husband, an absent and miserable father, and living a sinful life. This was another time that I was totally disgusted with my life and what I had become. What I had become was in complete contradiction of what I had idealized and envisioned for myself.

I was taught to believe in the power of prayer. (Thank God!) Even though I was not going to church and was carrying on a depraved life, I always remembered to pray. I would pray before I left home for God's mercy and keeping, even as I was involved in wicked deeds. I even prayed to God while I was throwing out the dice (praying for a win), all the while knowing in my heart that neither I nor my prayer was pleasing to God.

Time went by and I became increasingly dissatisfied with who I had become. I was doing things that, as a child and young man, I declared never to do. Again, I hated myself and what I had become, but was entrapped and unable to separate and deliver my soul from the enslavement of sin. I did not know what to do, but I believed with all my heart that God hears and answers prayers.

Even now, as I share my depraved and abject comportment of my life in writing, I can see in retrospect the trickery of Satan. Every time I thought of doing better and reversing my life, there would be an emergence of good fortunes in my favor. My "fun times" were pronounced, and I walked away from the dice table with more winnings than usual. Satan used the ploy of winning to keep me coming back, while at the same time giving me contentment with a ruinous existence.

I made myself content with who I was and what I had become, but there was also an inward disturbance of dissatisfaction. An incident happened (that I prefer not to reveal) to me at a Saturday-night ruckus that brought a change in my thinking. I will never forget when that Saturday-night event broke into a Sunday-morning transformation. I left my weekend hangout with evil intentions in mind, but by the time I arrived home, I was in a new mindset: I can do better than this! My "fun time" had miraculously become an overpowering period of depression.

I will forever remember that solemn time of sitting in my car, seemingly unable to pull myself away to go into the house. I don't know how long I sat out there in that solitude, but I am thankful for the conclusion. I distinctly remember contemplating my life from the innocence of my childhood to the disgust of that present time. I experienced grief, a sense of failure, regret, filth, and a horde of other emotions while I sat numb because of what I saw at that moment.

I remained stupefied in deep mental agitation in my car, when all of a sudden, I started to talk aloud to myself. I recall some of the things I said to myself in that intense soliloquy. I said to myself (to the best of my memory), "What are you doing out here like this? You were raised better than this! Your mama and daddy trained you better than this! You have a good wife who loves you, two children, a good job—what are you doing out here, living this life and doing the things you are doing?"

After my monologue I spread both hands on the steering wheel and laid my head between my hands. I have no idea how long I sat in my car or remained lifeless in this position. I do remember, however, feeling petrified in a frozen state of mind and body. It was as if I were paralyzed in time, suspended there, unable to free myself from motionlessness. It was as if I had to, or better yet was forced to, examine "me." I sat helpless to raise my head or use my hands to pry myself up from this frightful posture.

I began to perspire—no, that's too mild a terminology, I started to sweat profusely! My sweat glands gave out wet secretions from every orifice of my body (at least, it felt like it). I could not scream out for help or even rise up to lay on the horn to bring attention to anybody who would come to my rescue. It was a horrifying experience, leaving me to fear in wonderment as to whether I was about to die without being able to say my farewells to loved ones and friends. I was fretful, unable to move, wondering what was happening within me. *What's happening here, what's going on in my body? I have never felt like this; I've never experienced anything like this in my lifetime.* I came to the conclusion, in my mind, that I must be on the brink of having a stroke or heart attack.

How long I remained in my car in this state I cannot ascertain; only God knows. However, this I do remember—I snapped out of it and frantically broke out into uncontrollable tears. I can't say if they were tears of joy or tears of sadness; all I know is I was crying for no rhyme or reason. *What is happening to me, am I going crazy, am I losing my mind?* I didn't know what was going on, but one thing I was sure of—it was scary!

After the completion of this dramatic episode, I gathered myself and went into the house. My heart was accelerating with heavy, pounding beats as I pondered all that had previously happened. It was frightful just thinking about it. I quietly entered our bedroom, where my wife was sleeping, and sat on the side of the bed, still in deep concentration of the matters that had befallen me this night.

I don't know if the depression from my sitting on the mattress woke my wife or if it was a spiritual affair that called her to alertness. All I can attest to is that she woke up. I apologized for disturbing her and encouraged her to go back to sleep.

My wife, sensing something was wrong, asked what was bothering me. I don't know what prompted her to keep at it, but she was persistent in inquiring about my mental agitation. I couldn't comprehend it then, however, since that time I have become convinced that she had a spiritual revelation that ultimately contributed to my spiritual commitment to God. The more I tried to compel her to go back to sleep, the more diehard she seemed to be in her interrogation.

Our conversation became spiritual as I turned the tables by asking if she was going to church today. My inquiry was really redundant, especially since I knew that excluding the unforeseen sickness of her or one of the children (or immediate coming of Jesus Christ), my wife would be in church. Though my question was foolish in nature, my wife assured me that going to church was at the top of her Sunday agenda.

I announced that I was going to church with her and the kids today. There was much discussion on my statement (since I had said it often in the past) and deliberation on causes that would prevent me from making good on my claim. In previous times I had told her I was going to church only to have my intentions thwarted by a friend's invitation that would take me in another direction. If that interruption did not take place, I would fabricate excuses of being tired and not wanting to fall asleep in church. Then, there was the ultimate defense of not having the proper attire.

My intentions for church attendance for this Sunday were different and absolute. I showered, got dressed, and went to church with my family. I must admit I felt a sense of apprehension and shame when I entered the building. However, my embarrassment was crushed by warm greetings, firm handshakes, loving embraces, warm hugs, and affectionate kisses. I also received complimentary expressions of delight to see me in church (without making me feel ashamed of my long absence). My church family demonstrated a Christian love that made it easy to come back into the fold. Once again, I came before the church and apologized for my fall from grace and unfaithfulness to God and them. Once again, my church forgave me and welcomed me back with the right hand of fellowship.

My family and I went home, ate our meal, and returned to church for evening services. It felt good, and I was filled with the gratifying satisfaction of being with my family in church praising God. After all, a husband and father should be the spiritual leader of his household. I've always known it was my rightful place and the correct thing for me to do. I just had not been there or done it. It felt good to be back once again!

7
GOING FORWARD AGAIN

Since rededicating myself to the Lord, I realized I had to make extreme and serious adjustments in my living activities as well. I made up my mind that I was going to live a life reflecting the indwelling of God's Holy Spirit and exemplary in showing a commendable Christian life. I am ready to serve the Lord, I am on the battlefield for my Lord, I will serve Him 'til I die! I've enlisted in the Christian Army, I'm a soldier of the Cross!

My every inclination was to please God and to honor His Son, Jesus Christ, through righteous living. I was ardent at this time in my commitment to the Lord, as I had (at least in my mind) done before. I felt I had to; I couldn't leave the Church and go back to my detestable ways. To retreat and return to the life I had publicly denounced would put me in a dishonorable position and Christ to open shame.

I prayed, read my Bible, and attended my church's Bible Study and prayer fellowship events regularly. I bought Bible study materials, watched chosen television programing, and joined Men's Bible groups in my church and other churches in the area as well. I was determined to grow in the stature and nurture of God's Word.

I spent most of my waking hours reading the Bible, commentaries, and Bible study books. It was helpful that my wife joined me in my quest and investigation of God's Word. I was part of a carpool and when I wasn't driving the thirty-six-or-so-mile trip, I was reading. Then, since I was blessed to have a job that only required four to five hours of actual labor time, I was allowed additional reading time. When I finished my work assignment I would go to the company's "Steel Shed" (building where steel was stored), where I was able to read without being disturbed. I attempted to start a Bible study with my coworkers, but it was not received well since they preferred playing cards. However, there were occasional visits from passing employees who would come to "talk" and/or even seek my advice on matters of life. There was an older man who came more often than anyone else, and we talked about God and His goodness in our lives. The man was an officer in his church and a man who loved the Lord. I enjoyed this special time alone talking with this Brother and fellowship with others for spiritual enlightenment. It felt good and added to the accomplishment of my spiritual growth. There were times when my coworkers knew where I would be and felt comfortable enough to come to me for advice, or just a listening ear.

God is so good to allow a person the blessings of spiritual expansions and maturity in His Word to all who sincerely desire it. I have learned that in all relationships with God, it is a matter of Divine inspiration with human cooperation. God wants us to know Him in an intimate and embracing relationship. His Word encourages the reader/believer to constant, intensified inspiration and Bible study. Again, Divine inspiration with human cooperation. God gives His Word and inspiration, but it is up to each person to open up her or his Bible for reading and studying. It is like that in all phases of life; it is a matter of Divine inspiration with human cooperation. If a person would have greens in a garden, she or he has to prepare the soil, fertilize the ground, pluck up the weeds, and plant the seeds. In conjunction with Divine inspiration (wisdom), God will germinate the seed, and send the sunshine and rain to produce vegetation.

I felt good about myself and my augmented advancement in the knowledge of God's Word. I was gratefully amazed at how God was blessing me in understanding and retention of the things I read from the printed pages. And then, to top it all, I received complimentary accolades from people in my church, at my job, and in my community. I don't think I allowed pride to overtake my mind, but I have to be truthful and admit it made me feel good while I was in the glamour of attention.

Things in my life, mentally, physically, and spiritually, were good. I was studying and growing in God's Word. I was going to church every Sunday, participating in midweek church activities, staying home with my family, and getting our financial woes under control. I didn't have to say much about my faith, as others were talking about me and my beliefs.

My church had Sunday School with segregated classes for adult women and men. If a young adult came to Sunday School, she or he would have to sit in a class of his or her gender. I attended Sunday School and had to sit with the elderly, who discussed the biblical text but did not seem to bring out points that met my needs. I was a young man and wanted to be surrounded by my peers, people of my own age group, in talking about the Scriptures and how they could be applied to our everyday lives. I must point out that there were not a lot of young adults who attended Sunday School, even though we had received appeals and encouragement from our pastor from the pulpit about the need for Sunday School attendance. Despite the pastoral plea, it fell on deaf ears and only a few adhered to his request (and those who did only lasted for a short-lived stint).

There was a burning desire in my heart and mind to get a Young Adult Sunday School Class started. I prayed often, petitioning the Lord about my desire. I felt my inspiration was from God. I didn't get much out of the lessons amidst the older gentlemen where, for the most part, the class period was spent by the older Brothers giving their thoughts on the verses. It entered my mind to stop coming altogether and do as the rest of my age group—just don't come. However, there was a surge of celestial energy that wouldn't let me quit. After all, I had come back to the Church and made a statement of faith before all that were present. I've started, I've come back, I can't stop now; I must go forward. I felt, as I alluded to in an earlier statement, that all matters of life are inspired by Divine inspiration to be carried out through means of human cooperation.

Having all these thoughts and desires within, I found myself in something of a spiritual strait. I felt the need and prayed about the need. The constancy of my prayers resulted in an unction to do something about my desire in having a Young Adult Sunday School Class. There was a nagging notion before me to do something about it, to make it happen, and I couldn't shake it.

After a few weeks of this back-and-forth self-debating

and arguing, I knew I had to advance my desire. Before I did anything, I went to the Men's Sunday School teacher, a man I had come to love and respect. This dear Brother was a faithful and ardent student of God's Word. A person would have to love and respect his charismatic character and personality. I knew I had to handle this situation gingerly and cautiously. I did not and would not purposely do anything to hurt this great soul.

I wanted to be prudent in my actions and so, after much prayer, I made an appointment with my esteemed Brother in his home. When I explained my purpose in coming to him, I was amazed and gratefully astounded by his response. This grand old stalwart of my day told me my desire was an answer to his longtime prayer. This Brother gave me a stimulating approval and warm endorsement to be immediate in doing that which was in my mind.

My next step was to go to my pastor, which was the first of such an event in my life. I had never had a one-on-one consultation with any pastor. I made an appointment and met (fearfully, I must admit) with my pastor and revealed to him the things occupying my mind. I further proceeded to apprise him of my meeting with the Men's Sunday School teacher and his response. I was thrown back in utter amazement from the pastor. It was as if he were expecting my call and appointment before I made it. The pastor made it very easy for me to communicate my mission. This is significant for me, again, since I had never had a one-on-one encounter with a man of God, much less my pastor.

Now, after these many years and looking back in retrospect, I can see how this venerable, wily, Godly man took advantage of a young, inexperienced, newly rededicated member of the church (I write this in respectful jest). When I left this meeting, not only was my impulse readily received, but I was suggested by pastoral endorsement to be the teacher of the proposed new Young Adult Sunday School Class.

The Young Adult Sunday School Class was started at First Baptist Church, Vine Street, Malvern ("God's Country"), Arkansas, with Billy Blackmon as the first teacher. This teaching assignment was really good for me. I left my pastor inspired and committed to do a great work for the Lord through Sunday School. I bought books on teaching methods and techniques by renowned Sunday School teachers and authors. Most of my thoughts during this time were consumed with plans and methods of teaching to make the lessons alive and vibrant. I used the phone and made personal visits to tell my contemporaries of the good news in having a Sunday School class formulated just for us. Those I talked to and invited expressed delight in the news and assured me they would be there.

However, when the anticipated Sunday arrived, there were only three in the class: me, my wife, and one other person. I was deeply hurt and disgusted with the attendance, but tried not to let the disappointment show to the two female students. I gave my all in bringing out the lesson meaning and how we could apply it to our daily lives. The Words of Jesus are as appropriate today as when He first spoke them: "For where two or three are gathered together in My Name, there I Am in the midst of them" (Matthew 18:20 (NIV)). The Lord honored my efforts and our gathering and we felt His presence. He blessed us with a fruitful and helpful lesson explanation.

Even though I was disenchanted and discouraged with the attendance of the class, I refused to let the Devil have the victory. When those who had assured me they would be in Sunday School arrived for Morning Worship, I approached them. I was careful not to let my anger and hurt show. I simply informed them that I had missed them in our Sunday School class and hoped they would make it next Sunday. For the most part, the excuse offered was that they overslept and/or got up late. With all that was within me, I lovingly suggested that they set their alarm clocks to wake them up.

Although I recommended and encouraged the setting of alarms, I purposely called them on Saturday evening reminding them of their Sunday School commitment for the next morning. I even offered wake-up calls, but had no takers since they confirmed that they would be there. I jokingly (yet in earnest) promised that if they were not there tomorrow, they could look forward to a wake-up call the following Sunday morning. I said it in jest, but it was in my heart to do what I said. I planned to be persistent in reminding them. In my heart I was determined not to give up, and if they did not show up on the strength of their word, they would show up to silence my voice and nuisance. I was adamant in my pursuit to get them to come at least one time and was ready to do whatever necessary to get them there. There was no shame in my game!

I prayed before and after each call, asking the Lord to bless them to receive my invitation and to be able to rise the next morning to keep their word. I requested my wife to pray with me the night before we went to bed. We prayed fervently with great zeal for the class and the attendance.

It was an anxious and restless night for me in waiting for the morning light. However, since I could not sleep, I used the waking time to pray. When the dawning of that Sunday morning broke through, I got up with mixed emotions and thoughts. While getting ready and waiting for my family to get dressed, I was in constant prayer. Before leaving home, we had a family prayer. My wife and children prayed for the class and me. It was especially uplifting to hear my small children pray for their daddy. That in itself encouraged my heart.

God heard and answered our prayers! We were blessed with the presence of His Holy Spirit; we had a great time! There were questions, explanations, and terrific class participation. After we finished the lesson, I asked for and allowed expressions of the class and my teaching method. I appealed to the class for candid assessments on my lesson presentation, assuring them it would help serve my cause. I confessed to them that I wanted to be the best teacher I possibly could be. The expressions were all positive and encouraging. The attendees told me I had brought out things they had never seen before and how it applied to their lives. One Brother even stated that if he had known Sunday School was this interesting, he would have been coming all the time. By the way, if anyone is interested, there were thirteen present in class that day. Praise the LORD!

As may well be known, I was grateful and elated to witness the power and wonders of God. I was on a spiritual high, and boy, did it feel good! This teaching assignment was really good for me. It generated within me a greater compulsion to study and be ready for class. I read at home in the evenings, I studied the lesson going to work (when I wasn't driving, naturally), and at work. I was determined to be prepared before my class each Sunday morning. My objective, when I stood before others, was to be more informed about the lesson than anyone else. I was not going to let it be said (and true) that the Young Adult Class was not being taught. I even purchased Bible commentaries and other Bible helps. It was my goal to make each lesson explosive and relevant to life applications. I wanted to grow mentally and spiritually, and wanted all who attended our Young Adult Sunday School Class to grow also.

Although it was not my intention to build up a reputation as a teacher, it happened. I was blessed to hear outside testimonies of the lessons and my teaching proficiency. I'd be lying if I said I didn't like hearing those remarks. I was extremely delighted and encouraged when I would go into the barber shop and hear of what someone had said of my teaching (the remarks were complimentary). I cannot put into words how good that made me feel. In my mind I was where God wanted me to be, doing what God wanted me to do, and hopefully saying what God wanted me to say. Things were going well for me, and I was thankful for all God was doing in my life and through me. The God of all was using me, and I liked it! I felt so special, and although I knew it wasn't the case, it felt like God had forgotten everyone else in the world and was focusing on me only. That's the kind of God we serve; He's so wonderful and personal that He makes all feel like she/he is special.

Things were indeed going well for me. I was in church teaching a Sunday School class, growing in God's Word, and loving every minute of it. I knew I was in the good pleasures of the Lord, helping to edify the saints of God and doing what I should be doing for His cause. I was on my way to fulfilling the destined plan and blueprint of God for my life. I present this fact not in a boastful fashion, but humbly to give God the glory of what He will do if a person will give over to Him completely in His service. It was obvious that I was on an upward path. I was going forward with no desire to turn back!

8
SAME FOLK

The story is told of a pastor of a small church in a rural town where everybody knew everybody else. The pastor owned a parrot that needed caring for while he attended a pastor's conference in a neighboring state. The pastor was able to get one of the deacons of the church to tend to the parrot while he was away. The pastor informed the deacon that the parrot loved church gatherings and didn't fit in well in other places and environments.

However, at the close of the week, the deacon needed to unwind by going to a local nightclub. The deacon sat near the club entrance and sat the parrot on his perch. They were sitting in a position that afforded them the opportunity to see anyone who came into the club.

A short time after arriving at the club a group piled in through the doors. Seeing the crowd, the parrot shouted out, "Church! Church!"

The deacon quickly quieted the parrot by telling him they were in a club, not a church.

A few minutes later and another group of people came through the doors. Seeing the crowd, the parrot squawked out, "Church! Church!"

Again, the deacon reminded the parrot he was not in a church and that he had to be quiet.

No sooner than the deacon had gotten the words out of his mouth, another crowd entered the premises, and sure enough, the parrot bellowed out, "Church! Church!"

The deacon angrily scolded the parrot, telling him, "Look, I told you, we're in a club, not a church, so shut up!"

The bird was quiet until another group herded their way into the building. True to his nature, the parrot immediately yelled out, "Church! Church!"

The deacon again chided the bird by telling him, "Listen, this is the last time I'm telling you, we're in a club, we're not in church!"

The parrot quickly responded, "Same folk! Same folk!"

Things were truly going well with me. I was content with what I had and where I was in life. I had stable employment with good pay, I was actively involved in my family's lives, and my spiritual participation (church-going) was paramount. I don't think I've ever felt more fulfilled or complete.

Although I felt accomplished and was experiencing a state of bliss, I have to be honest and confess there were some episodes of restlessness. I would occasionally run into someone who was part of my past social circle. They would express delight in seeing me and then follow up with a statement or question concerning my whereabouts and what I had been doing. They would talk about the world I had withdrawn from and would use descriptive language that welled up nostalgic and wistful cravings. As I've said before, Satan is the master of deception and will use any means necessary to pull a person into his web of deceit. I could not see it then and was not aware of his evil duplicity, but boy, was he ever present!

About a year or so after I came back to the Church and recommitted my life to the Lord, things seem to have come from all sides to entice me back into depravity. It was with more regularity that I would run into people of the arena of my past excursions. When I left their company, I would feel loneliness and an aching for my former cohorts. Come on, Satan, will you never cease to bother me?

I was able to overcome my anxieties and emotions by praying and fasting. It was an extremely hard time for me. I had many people I could have gone to in confidence to share my weakness, but Satan prevented that from happening. The Devil kept before me my past and how if I would confess my faults, people would deem me weak and incompetent. That rascal would keep me in remembrance of former times when I strayed from God and His Church. I had come before them in repentance in the past, and I just couldn't let that happen again.

I knew my thoughts and compulsions were not of God and fought those diabolical impressions with every fiber of my mortal being. I read, prayed, and fasted more frequently during these distressing times. I was perplexed as to why I was having these awful thoughts and desires, especially when I didn't want to. After all, I was living, to the best of my ability, a righteous life. I was reading and studying the Bible extensively, praying much, and fasting often. I needed and was moved to get a greater comprehension and deeper understanding of why I was going through this traumatic experience.

This was the scenario I surmised from the scant evidence and information set before me. It was a fact that God and I both well knew. I wanted to live an exemplary life of righteousness before Him. I was truly in a contrite frame of mind when I returned to the Lord via my confession before His Church. I was living and modeling my deportment by the instructions I gathered from His Word. I was not perfect and was still struggling with some unsavory habits that I greatly wanted to abandon and was working toward their dissolution. I had made God's Word the primary focus of my private reading and studying. I made sure to keep myself mentally equipped to maintain the teaching of a God-blessed (in growth and learning) Sunday School class. I had also ascribed myself to the practice of committed prayer and fasting.

I knew I was positively growing spiritually and felt the presence of the Holy Spirit within me. So, the prevalent question ever present before me was, "Why is all this happening to me?"

Friends of my past seemed to pop out of the woodwork to tell me how much they missed me while extending an invitation to come back and join the fellowship. Some of them would use the permissive statement of persuasion, "I know you're in church now, but it won't hurt you to come around every now and then." These words would prolong their persuasive presence in my mind as a later tool for Satan to use against me. I didn't realize the potency of that suggestion and the percussion it would place on me later.

As I stated earlier, life was good to me, and I was happy in the Lord. I had come back to the Lord and His Church. Since that time, I had been staying at home with my family, therefore I was wasting less money. When I no longer ravaged the family budget and income, it naturally resulted in more money in our account. My conscience was clear, so I had a peace of mind. God was extremely good to me, and things seemed to coordinate in sync with my needs, both physically and spiritually.

Transitions in my life have given me a more emphatic understanding of the predicaments of the biblical character Job. Job was a resident in the land of Uz and was blessed of God to possess immense wealth. Job was highly favored in the eyes of Almighty God, then unbeknownst to Job he was allowed, by the permissive will of God, to be tested by the Devil. When this permission was granted, Job's life and fortunes were instantly abducted with absolute loss and health failure. All of this came upon Job with no warning.

At the risk of being redundant, as I stated previously, during this period of my life, things were going good for me. I felt a closeness to God I had never experienced before through and by His Word. My relationship with my family was healthy and beneficial for us all. God had blessed me to successfully bring again my finances into check and under control. I was in church, reading and studying my Bible, and teaching a Sunday School class—life was great! I felt God's blessings and favor over all of my life.

I cannot pinpoint specifically the exact time and date, but in the midst of all the veneration of blessings, adverse circumstances came abruptly upon me. Out of nowhere, with no foreseen warning at all, my life was turned upside down, from good to bad, from blessings to curses. I can testify from experience that life is uncertain and will change in a moment. When a person is blindsided by misfortune, when life turns sour and goes south, the changes can be constant, continuous, and challenging.

Looking back, I impute the beginning of my complications to the conversations with my friends of my past. I evidently, no matter how unwittingly, listened to what I was being told by my former familiars and it remained with me. They expressed how much they wanted to see me, and in my heart (being truthful), I longed to be with them. Their words of encouragement to join them would always haunt me later when I was left alone with the rudiments of my thoughts and their words. I have to confess and re-emphasize that their statements appealed to my inner intellect and desires. I had avoided and walked away from the things I was convicted to be wrong for Christians to be partakers of.

However, as much as I hate to admit it and confess (then and now), I was a Christian with sinful inclinations. Like Apostle declares in Romans 7:18a (KJV), "For I know that in me (that is, in my flesh) dwelleth no good thing." I came to the knowledge of knowing that, in my body, were the abodes of good and evil. I wanted to live a good and righteous life, while at the same time, gratify the lust and avarice of the flesh. In my body were two natures, warring one against the other, one to the good and one to the bad, both attempting to conquer my soul. This indeed is a mixture of good and bad, as I am the "Same folk! Same folk!"

This chapter will endeavor to express the depth of my frustration with my quandary. My whole being (mental, physical, and spiritual) was affected during this epoch of my life. I was, in my personal view and estimation, in a bad fix and knew not what to do to deliver myself out of this body of death.

Satan had so orchestrated that my old friends and I would inconspicuously, but conveniently, meet and greet. The conversation was virtually always the same. I would be graciously greeted, given lament for the lack of seeing me in recent times, and a warm invitation to mix company with them again. These invitations would appeal to the vile side of me, making me pine away with guilt at the same time.

My problem was that when I left their presence, their

words took root in my mind and thoughts. I had to remind myself of my contentment and satisfaction that I had reclaimed in the Lord, and that my disassociation was the right thing to do. I felt better about myself and the concerns of the life I had left behind. I could never return to the culpable habits and behavior I had declared never to do again. The temptations were alluring, but I kept reminding myself of what such association would do. I just couldn't do it; it would be detrimental and shameful. I would put myself, the Church, and Jesus Christ to open shame. I couldn't let it be said that I was insincere and hypocritical. No! No way could I let that happen.

However, as the adage goes, "Never say never!" I wrestled with myself and my conscience. There was an inner warfare trying to pull me in two opposite directions at the same time. A part of me wanted to defect and give in to the urges of my flesh and the former courses of my life. On the other hand, a small, still voice inwardly kept warning me of the consequences that would surely come if I gave in to my sinister preferences. I was viciously vexed as to what I should do. I wanted to have fun by rejoining my pragmatic acquaintances, but at the same time, I knew that was not the right thing to do. In my mind I was confronted with the Word of the Lord quoted by Apostle Paul in 1 Corinthians 6:12: "All things are lawful unto me, but I will not be brought under the power of any." Then, as the Lord would have it, the Holy Spirit also brought to me the writing in 1 Corinthians 10:22 where Paul repeats the doctrine of good warfare: "All things are lawful for me, but all things are not expedient: all things are lawful, but all things edify not."

I could never adequately put into words the vehement forces that were housed within my body and mind. What a spiritual war it was taking place inside me. I wanted to go simultaneously in both directions. Desiring to do good and evil, I found myself fitted in the descriptive terminology of the parrot in the story—I was truly the "Same folk! Same folk!"

I was definitely in a spiritual warfare, battling for my soul. There was indeed a conflict where I was left torn in every aspect of my being. Paul declared a fact that I found to be infallibly true when he wrote in Ephesians 6:12, "For we wrestle not against flesh and blood, but against principalities, against powers, against the rulers of the darkness of this world, against spiritual wickedness in high places." I certainly agree with the Apostle, as Satan led an all-out battle within my mental and spiritual compositions. I was acutely aware that I was in an unphysical struggle, but my problem was in calculating a defense.

So, here I was, literally in a fight for my soul. I wanted, in my mind, to live a life of righteousness to the best of my ability to the glory of God. My greatest wish was to live such a Godly life that others would take notice of my Jesus imitation and would also want to live to His honor and directives. This was in my heart and psyche to accomplish, so why was it so hard? I knew I wanted to live for God in such a way that as I follow Jesus, others would want to follow my example as a child of God. I wanted more than anything else in this world to epitomize and be an example of a disciple of Jesus Christ. But alas, the truth of the matter was within and shouted out loudly in my spiritual ears, "Same folk! Same folk!"

The thoughts filling my mind caused a pandemonium beyond my ability to express. I knew I was facing distressing situations beyond me. What could I do to escape this private warfare that clearly had me devastated? All I knew told me it wasn't supposed to be this way; I'm a new creation. I'm living for Christ Jesus! So again, the question begged to be answered, "So, why am I having these evil longings?" I needed to know why I was yearning to return to my old ways. Why was I missing and desiring the habits I left behind and now looked upon as repugnant? I sincerely wanted to live a holy life, free of evil, devoid of unholy ways; so why was I being hassled by the fact that I was the "Same fold! Same folk!"

I struggled greatly with this. I didn't have an immediate solution to set right the problem. Seeking a counteraction to my crisis, I gave myself to inward thought as I sought my choice of actions. Of course, one option was to give myself to prayer and ask God for direction and the power to resist. If anyone would be able to guide me, it would be the God Who has an answer for any and all arduous situations incumbent to this life.

I straightway gave myself to persistent prayer. If there was ever a time in my life when I needed direction from the Lord, the time had surely come and the time was now. Having learned and known the power of God and His delight in hearing the prayers of His children, I not only prayed, but I also gave myself to periods of fasting.

Looking back on that critical time in my life, I was doing something unconsciously that worked in my favor. In my private reading of the Bible, a daily habit I had formed, the Book of Psalms revealed some vital strength that brought answers and inspiration. I needed to be heard by God, and I needed Him to hear and answer my pleas quickly. I was deprived of knowing what to do, and waiting patiently has never been one of my strong suits. I was like a commercial that was popular around that time: "I need help and I need it now!" I needed God and I needed Him now! I'm in trouble, I need the Lord to help me in resisting these irresistible and constant urges that make me cry out in tearful desperation and admission, "I am the same folk! Same folk!"

Frustrated and disgusted with myself, and having no immediate power to overcome my afflictions, I became prey for Satanic apprehension. The Deceiver beguiled me with the age-old generational ploy that "going out with the guys" every now and then can't do much harm. For, after all, I could witness to them, since it would only be an occasional occurrence. What could be so wrong with that? I would be with my friends who missed me, and I certainly missed them. After all, I could have fellowship with them and also tell them about the Lord. BIG LIE FROM THE PITS OF HELL! I was on the verge of backsliding and reverting to old ways. As much as I hate to say it about the man I was becoming, I was the "Same folk! Same folk!"

Convincing myself that it would be all right, I made my first recursion to past routines. I will never forget that planned Friday evening. I used the term "planned" purposely, as that is precisely what I did. I chose Friday deliberately over the other six days of the week so as not to be seen hanging out in forbidden places on Saturday night and showing up on Sunday morning teaching a Sunday School class. It would at least give the people who saw me a day or two to forget they had seen me. Yeah, Friday would definitely be the most strategic day to go and do my sneakiness. Old Satan is a pro in supplying reasons and excuses for committing misdeeds.

The first outing was charged with emotional and harrowing guilt. I felt remorseful of what I had done, and my conscience did not give me the luxury of leaving me alone in peace. I was reprehensive and filled with boundless grief over my weekend digressions. Then, to complicate things and make matters worse, everyone I met and knew caused a state of paranoia to set in. Thoughts like *They know* and *They're talking about me* ate me up inside, increasing my guilt complex. Once I left that atmosphere, I promised myself I would never do that again. However, the closer the weekend came, the more I entertained going out to repeat my adventures. I chastised myself for allowing my thoughts and concentrations to be filled with this wickedness. How could I let myself come to this? That meddling voice within reminded me I was the "Same folk! Same folk!"

Although I promised to myself I was not going to let my compulsions draw me back into a life of indecency, it was easier said than done. At the close of each work week there seemed to well up in me a massive urge to go out, to unwind, and to enjoy myself. For, after all, I deserved a little fun; everybody else does. The thought that ran through my mind was that even the Scriptures teach that a person is entitled to benefit from the fruits of his or her labor. So, why was it so wrong for me to go out and have a little fun? I shouldn't feel so bad about that.

I was successful in convincing myself that my feelings and actions were perfectly normal and I was no worse for them. After all, I wasn't hurting anyone, it wasn't like I was committing murder or some big sin. Then, when I observed the crowd, I noticed other people who went to church were present also. So, why should I feel bad about myself when people in all denominations were doing the same thing I was doing? I saw it as a sort of a Mexican standoff— "You don't say anything about what I'm doing and I won't say anything about what you're doing." We were, for the most part, congregants of some church in Malvern ("God's Country") and its surroundings. We were all blameworthy, and it could be said of all of us, "Same folk! Same folk!"

This is the mental placebo that the Devil presented for me to soothe my conscience in justifying my cause. Now, I am able to go out and have a change of scenery and routine without the burden of relentless guilt. And then, there's always that proverbial truth, "the more you do a thing, the easier it is to do." I was bothered less with each successive week of my extracurricular relaxations. I was mindful, however, to minimize my outings to Friday evening since I would be standing before my Sunday School class on Sunday morning. This action was based on the theory "out of sight, out of mind." If the people did not see me on Saturday night, by Sunday morning they would have forgotten completely about seeing me on Friday night.

During this unsettled time of my life, I read Romans, chapter one, and saw myself vividly. Paul wrote in Romans 1:26a, "For this cause God gave them up to vile affections." Then, he continued further down in Romans 1:28, "And even as they did not like to retain God in their knowledge, God gave them over to a reprobate mind, to do those things which are not convenient."

As powerful as God is, He will never force Himself on anyone. If humans are to serve, praise, or do God's bidding, it is because a person of her or his own free will or volition chooses to follow His determined course of life. The more I frequented the "fun places," the less my conscience condemned me. It is of a fervent truth that if a person chooses to participate in a life of salacious activities, God will allow him or her to be in control of their actions. Although it may hurt our heavenly Father, He respects and gives everyone the privilege of choice. We can either be a person of Godly change or we can be the "Same folk! Same folk!" God gives the referendum to each individual, but warns all that if a person elects to abide in sin and hypocrisy, He will give that person over to his or her decision.

This is where I was at in this intersection of my life. I wanted, with every fiber of my being, to live a life of purity that would honor God and edify humanity by displaying a commitment to righteousness (in Jesus's Name) that others could emulate. Yet, here I was, being what I didn't want to be and doing things I despised. Oh, wretched man that I am! I am truly a person of sinful tendencies. Like the assessment of the parrot in the story when he blatantly and truthfully proclaimed, "Same folk! Same folk!"

Then, if my inner emotions and convictions were not enough, some insipid and tasteless remarks concerning my character and Christian living were being circulated. It was brought to my attention that it was rumored that I was a hypocrite and was doing things that Christians shouldn't do. People are always going to say bad remarks about a person who tries to live for the Lord, but when it is true, it is a sad commentary. It was bad enough to have that report said about me in my city, but now the assassination of my character had spilled over to my workplace. I was made aware that one of the men in my carpool had commented that I was still doing what I used to and there was no change in my life and habits. The rumors deemed me to be the "Same folk! Same folk!"

I was devastated by the statements railed against me. But to be candid, the truth hurts. I didn't like what was being said, I even detested hearing it; however, truth is not relative but absolute, and it does not change. Regardless of any distaste I may have harbored in not wanting to hear the negative accusations, it was still true as a reminder to me that I was admittedly the "Same folk! Same folk!" With all that I was facing and encroaching, I remembered a statement I heard from my mother and in a sermon by my pastor: "If you don't like what is being said about you and it's true, stop doing it."

Oh, what a disgusted state of delirium I found myself to be in. Lord, why have I allowed myself this lot in life? Then, in a turn of mental and spiritual embattlement, I turned to God. I questioned my Creator in seeking reasons for my inability to live a holy and upright life. Why, Lord, am I like this? In retrospect, I probably accused God of allowing me to fall to this low point of existence and doing nothing to prevent my deplorable state.

There are times when present unpleasant quandaries won't let a person see the visible blessings before her or him. In my daily Bible reading in the Book of Psalms, God was answering, but I was not able to recognize it at that particular time. I didn't know it then, but in hindsight, I am more than convinced that my Heavenly Father was trying to teach and show His weak child that everything I needed was in His Word. The power I desired and craved was readily available in the Scriptures. All I needed was in the confines of His Word, and I knew it not.

How blind I was! I was miserable and afflicted, devoid of what to do. I was in a state of regression and had fallen back into my old ways of life. I had entered back into depravity, and the worst part about it was that I was enjoying it—a lot! The questions that filled and occupied my thoughts were: *Why did I let this happen? Where was God, and why did He allow me to return to my former distasteful ways?* Apostle Peter could have had me in mind when he wrote in 2 Peter 2:22 (KJV), "But it happened unto them according to the true proverb, the dog is turned to his own vomit again, and the sow that was washed to her wallowing in the mire." This verse fit me to the tee—I was, like it or not, the "Same folk! Same folk!"

The problem that perplexed me most was, "How did this happen? How had I lost control?" The old man is presumably supposed to be dead, and dead men can do no wrong. When had the old man been resurrected from the abyss of the depths of the grave to overpower the new creation? All I knew was that there was indeed a relapse in my life to render me to a subsistence of reality—I was the "Same folk! Same folk!"

I didn't know how to correct my situation, but I knew that a change had to take place. I was downtrodden and depressed that I had allowed my life to come full circle to a state I said I would never return to again. I hated myself for relapsing into a being I had thought was dead and out of the way. I want him dead forever; what can I do to keep the old man deceased with no possibility of rising again? The old man was dead. I witnessed his death through a new creation in Christ Jesus. I was, though saved, plagued by the ghost of the flesh and mind that had condensed me again into the right judgment of the parrot in the story. I was the "Same folk! Same folk!"

9
WHAT TO DO, WHAT TO DO

It was at this juncture of my life that I now feel (as I did then) that God was initiating a lasting and perpetual lesson that would serve useful to me in my spiritual life and growth. God, even though I did not see it at the time, was revealing to me a spiritual ecstasy into His good grace. Jehovah God met me at the point of my need in my spiritual maturation that proved successful for me then as well as for subsequent times in the future.

It was at this time that my daily reading/mediation was in the Book of Psalms and this awesome God of heaven and earth began His revelatory work in me. Here I was, discouraged with myself and disgusted because I had recoiled into a regression by permitting unwanted habits to control my actions. I did not like where I was or what I had become. And, to make matters worse, the constant reverberating voice of my conscience was screaming out, "What am I to do? What am I to do in going forward?"

In my daily self-enrichment of the Scriptures in the King James Version of the Bible, I started to see new oracles. It was as if I were reading the book for the first time. I felt that I was initiated into new inspirations and enlightenment. The irony of it all was that although I had read the verses before, they all of a sudden were giving me new insight. The things I was currently reading were miraculously filled with messages that I needed at that time. In the Book of Psalms I learned that the Psalmist was much like me, in trouble and lost as to what to do to get out of his unpleasant circumstances. In the Book of Psalms I saw that the Psalmist experienced similar passions to what I was enduring.

The verses seemed to prodigiously jump out at me right before my eyes. They had been there all the time, but the time had not yet come for the Holy Spirit to reveal the message to me. With total disappointment with my life and spiritual imperfections, I was ready to give up. I was at the point of abandoning any effort to live a Christian life at all. What was the use? Everything I was doing was heading downward and spiraling out of control; I was headed for a spiritual train wreck! Where was God in all this? He said He would never leave nor forsake me, so where was He? Why was all this happening to me? After all, He knows everything, so why was He not giving me the strength to live as I should? Why was He not supplying me with the withal to live a holy life and overcome this onslaught of evil desires and actions?

After wrestling with my pathetic situation and even (which I now know and confess) blaming God, I sought Him for the answer. I am the creation and child of God who truly wants to represent His holiness through righteous living. How did I get here and what can I do to get back on the right track? As I mused over my state of being, I concluded that I needed to cast all my cares on the Lord, since He cares for me. That's what His Word declares, and I'm in such a fatal fix, He's the only help I can envision. Thank God for the blessed privilege of being able to go to Him anytime.

Then, one day, like a bolt of lightning, it hit me! God opened my understanding and allowed me to see my needed answers in the very Book I was currently reading. I had always heard that God will meet you where you are, at the point of your need. That's apropos and germane of the character of the omnipotent God Who is all-powerful and ever-present. We ought, all of heaven and earth, especially those of us who confess Him, to praise God for His everlasting grace and mercy.

It all began in Psalms 69:17. I saw relativity in the Word of God that satisfied my present need and would subsequently enrich and bless my spiritual growth in the Lord. Psalm 69:13–18 (KJV) reads, "But as for me, my prayer is unto thee, O Lord, in an acceptable time: O God, as in the multitude of thy mercy hear me, in the truth of thy salvation. Deliver me out of the mire, and let me not sink: let me be delivered from them that hate me, and out of the deep waters. Let not the waterflood overflow me, neither let the deep swallow me up, and let not the pit shut her mouth upon me. Hear me, O Lord; for thy lovingkindness is good: turn unto me according to the multitude of thy tender mercies. And hide not thy face from thy servant; for I am in trouble; hear me speedily. Draw nigh unto my soul, and redeem it: deliver me from mine enemies."

Just when I needed it most, there it was—exactly the emergence I had to have for survival. It had been there all the time, right there before me. It was not hidden in a mythical, mysterious, obscure oracle, it was right there before me. I didn't have to go through an initiation or ritual, it was right there before my eyes. I did not require the assistance of a mediator, tutor, teacher, or interpreter; it was simple. In fact, it was so simple that a fool need not err. Thank You, Holy Father, for opening up Your Word to me. Thank you, Brother David, for alerting me to the fact that my feelings were not isolated to me only. This experience was the inception of my realization in knowing that everything I need to know can be found in the Word of God.

These verses suited my taste and encouraged me to read more in the Book of Psalms to see what the end would bring. I found profound help in the latter part of Psalms 69, verses 32 and 33, which read, "The humble shall see this and be glad: and your heart shall live that seek God. For the Lord heareth the poor, and despiseth not his prisoners." But then, as I was leaving the Psalm, verse 29 seemed to scream out to me: "I have something that will help you out also. . . . But I am poor and sorrowful: let thy salvation set me up on high."

After I finished this reading, I literally stopped to digest the words I had called out and was moved to think on them. I was further inspired to do a Scripture reference study in Psalms to see if there were any other gems of help in the Book I could glean. I'm so glad and thankful for the urging of the Holy Spirit to "search the Scriptures," for in them I found power for my weary mind and soul.

Now, I could just list them and let you, the reader, look up the verses for yourself; however, since you may not find the inclination, time, or desire to do so, I thought it would be more impactful and convenient to print the verses for you. After all, I was there anyway and can save you the trouble. These verses were most appropriate and an unmistakable expression of my inner feeling and appeals.

I was considerably desperate and needed the Lord if I was to overcome the turmoil of my mind. I certainly could relate to David in his uttered quote in Psalm 70:5, "But I

All I Need Is In God's Word

was poor and needy: make haste unto me, O God: thou art my helper my deliverer, O Lord, make no tarrying." I saw in these words of a struggling man the exact same sentiments that I was feeling at that particular time.

I was filled with helplessness and was in need of an outlet. My total being—physical, mental, and spiritual—was affected. I thank God for His unsearchable riches in wisdom and grace as He showed me other great verses in Psalms that gave me strength in a time of great weakness.

Psalm 71:1 and 2 lifted my spirit with its word offering: "In Thee O Lord, do I put my trust: let me never be put to confusion. Deliver me in Thy righteousness and cause me to escape: incline Thine ear to me." This verse was befitting and intricate to my situation in expressing my profound declaration for this time.

This stuff was good and it had been there all the time; I just didn't know it. It was right there in God's Word, awesome and available for me. I was tremendously helped as I gave careful reading to the following exerts from the Book of Psalms:

Psalm 77:7–9, "Will the Lord cast off forever? And will He be favorable no more? Is His mercy clean gone forever? Doth His promise fail for evermore? Hath He in anger shup up His tender mercy?"

Psalm 79:5, "How long Lord? Wilt Thou be angry forever? Shall Thy jealousy burn like fire?"

Psalm 85:5–7, "Wilt Thou be angry with us forever? Wilt Thou draw out Thine anger to all generations? Wilt Thou not revive us again; that Thy people may rejoice in Thee? Shew us Thy mercy, O Lord and grant us Thy salvation."

Psalm 88:1, 2, 13, and 14, "O Lord God of my salvation, I have cried night and day before Thee. Let my prayer come before Thee: incline Thy ear unto my cry, But unto Thee have I cried O lord, and in the morning shall my prayer prevent Thee. Lord why casteth Thou off my soul? Why hidest Thou Thy face from me?"

Psalm 102:1 and 2, "Hear my prayer O Lord, and; let me come unto Thee. Hide not Thy face from me in the day when I am in trouble; incline Thine ear to me: in the day when I call answer me speedily."

When I read and meditated afresh on these powerful verses of truth, I received a twofold blessing. Firstly, I was nurtured in knowing that another had gone through what I was presently experiencing. Secondly, I was invigorated by the fact that the help I needed had been right there before me all the time, right there in the Word of God.

Now then, since I had received inspiration and now felt hopeful spiritual vibrations, I found myself still in a dilemma. I had received divine motivation, but what was I to do? In an earlier declaration I stated a personal conviction. I believe with all my heart that life is filled with a series of divine inspiration coupled with human cooperation. So now, I found myself with the awesome task of deciding what was right. Oh, what to do? What to do?

I am sure most people will agree with me in assessing that life, with all its constant issues and knots, makes for a difficult existence. Every day of our lives we are castigated with not only internal battlement, but also external interferences that bring grief to a body. These dominant factors bring about uncomfortable and antagonistic conflicts that cannot be easily dismissed. Life forces upon each of us a desire to postpone such confrontations for as long as we can, and if possible, indefinitely, but they come. Oh, what to do! What to do!

Perhaps these uncomfortable conditions could be more durable if disharmony only magnified itself in a single aspect of life. However, to the contrary, there are devastating grapples in every nook and corner of life trying to conquer the soul. Situations of this unwarranted warfare are guaranteed for life. Disruptive uprisings hit us when least expected, for the most part, from all possible angles and circumstances. They appear and manifest themselves in every situation—physical, mentally, and spiritually.

When I consider the drudgeries and hurtful labors of life, I can readily empathize with the Bible patriot Jacob. In Genesis 42, Jacob is faced with an unenviable lot in life. Jacob felt that in addition to losing two sons, he was now being asked to give up a third one. This son was the youngest of twelve, the last to be birthed by his beloved wife. It was just too much to ask of the old patriarch. Parents live knowing that we will die, but the expectancy is that the children will outlive and bury the parents, not vice versa. In Jacob's mind, he would be bereaved of the two sons that had come from the womb of his favorite wife, Rachel.

Jacob, facing this unpleasant quandary, in Genesis 42:36 grimly states, "Me have you bereaved of my children: Joseph is not, and Simeon is not, and ye will take Benjamin away: all these things are against me." In modern vernacular of these contemporary times, it would be heard of Jacob, "Oh, what to do! What to do!"

It is my firm belief and conviction that all of the human race, if not now, will ultimately come face to face with life's perplexing sharpness of being alive. Regardless of race, gender, social status, or pedigree, every person will come to what I call a "What to do! What to do!" situation. The only way to avoid a collision with such an event is not to be born.

Continuing with my personal narrative, I come back to

my strait in life at that time. Here now, I was enjoying life—I had a good family life, was gainfully employed, was taking care of my family's needs (and wants), going to church regularly, and even teaching a Sunday School class. Things were going extraordinarily well for me in the physical realm.

However, I was doing admittedly little to accomplish what I really hungered for. I wanted to live a clean life, a life of holiness, a life that would set me apart. I yearned to live with a deep affection for maintaining a state of sanctification and living in purity. More than life itself, I had a vehement ambition to flourish in righteousness as much as possible for any human to achieve. I can truly attest that my aspirations were not ostentatious or rooted in vainglory. I just wanted to live a life that would bring honor and glory to God.

However, wanting and being can be altogether diametric to one another. Bringing your objectives into reality requires a might that is grossly beyond the smarts of human powers and nature. It just isn't a part of mortal composition. There are none who can boast of being sinless (and be telling the truth). No, not one!

So, here I was, seemingly in a vacuum, suspended and devoid of power or any understanding of what to do. All I knew at this time was that I wanted, more than anything else, to live an exemplary life for Jesus. I wanted to live in a way that would speak so loud to the glory of God it would be a compelling force in bringing others to the Lordship of Jesus Christ. My greatest obsession during this period of my life was to "Let my lights so shine before men that they may see my good works and want to glorify the Father Which is in heaven."

What a perplexing predicament I found myself in! Ready, willing, and highly desirous of a righteous existence, but unable to make it a reality. Wanting to portray the love of God through virtuous actions was the culminating apex of my life ambitions. I knew what I wanted, I knew what I wanted to do, I just didn't know how to bring it to futility. "Oh, what to do! What to do!"

My befuddlement began to wear on me and enrage me into a state of irritation and disappointment. I felt I was a failure and my confidence had abandoned me. I was experiencing a low I had never felt before. I wanted to be a Christian, but the truth of the matter was, nothing had really changed. I strove for godliness, but all efforts were derailed by countless episodes of failure and defections. At that point of my life, all that could be truthfully said of my spiritual quest was that I was a religious repugnant. I strove for godliness, but I was living a lie and doing the misdeeds I grossly abhorred. I was caught on a "going cycle"—going to work, going to the clubs, and going to church (and I might also add, going to hell!). Then, there was the Adversary, Satan, the Devil, ever present to constantly remind me of my hypocrisy.

The Devil is great in what he does when his victim attempts to fight him with human arms and resources. He will devour the person with every arsenal at his disposal, both of a physical aspect as well as from a spiritual counter. He will deceive by the uses of images and thoughts that turn the person's eyes from the Lord and look inward for help, which usually turns to self-detriment. Then, when he is done, he leaves the person blaming God for the predicament. A person is foolish when that person thinks she or he capable of accomplishing victory over the Devil on his or her own merits.

I pause here to challenge the mind of anyone who doesn't believe in a real and literal Devil. And, by the way, that is one of his most effective tools: to cause a person not to believe or give credence to the fact of his existence. If you really want to know the domineering power of Satan, I dare you (no, I double-dog dare you) to submit yourself to the Lordship of Jesus Christ with the purposeful intention of living a life of righteousness.

The Adversary will use all forms of subtleties and elective ways of accomplishing his evil guile. He disrupts the mind with deliberate intentions of bringing about adverse and inimical damages to the total composition of a person. The Devil does all he can to destroy the moral and fleshly constitution of the human makeup where God is concerned. Satan is ardently competent in confusing and throwing off track anyone with aspirations to live a life dedicated and committed to God. If you don't believe it, again I challenge you to seriously give yourself over to God through His Son, Jesus Christ. If you receive Him, you will find the presence and realness of both Almighty God and the Master of Deception, the Devil.

The Ruler of Darkness, Satan, Lucifer, the Prince of Evil, the Angel ousted from heaven, is the Adversary of Jehovah God. The Devil knows he will never be welcomed or allowed to the eternal heavenly throne and kingdom of God. The Evil One wants to pain the heart of the Eternal Creator. Satan knows the love of a heavenly Father Who loves all of His creative beings. The Evil One is well aware of God's love for humanity and how He gave His Only Begotten Son to die on the Cross for sinners. It is betwixt the fact that that old Serpent knows he will never be permitted entrance before God in favor and wants to break God's heart by deceiving His handiwork to commit sin.

The drudgery and complexity of it all makes even the most serious and ambitious want to throw up their hands and cry out, "Oh, what to do! What to do!"

10
FROM HERE TO THERE

Let me attempt to paint a picture of my station in life. Where I was did not match the ideal posture and demeanor I had in mind. I wanted to be a Christian, a good and faithful servant of God. My prayer and desire toward God was to be a reliable, sincere, and devoted follower of Jesus Christ. As a disciple of the Lord, I endeavored to live a life dedicated to truth and righteousness.

My goal was obvious, as truly I was ready and wanted to go forward in the Name of Jesus Christ. I knew what I wanted to do and be in representing Christianity and the practice of Godly theology. My objective was clear and defined in my mind as to what I wanted to be and where I wanted to go. My mission in life was abundantly transparent and clear. I knew well what I wanted to be and accomplish. That part was easily assessed and expressed with crystal clarity. However, the problem was in the actualization of my impulses to make them a reality.

At this juncture of my life, I didn't have an inkling as to how or what to do to bring about the radical results I yearned for in my distorted life. I now realize, in hindsight, that the confusion I was experiencing was overpowering, to say the least. It came to the point of a disrupted tragedy that left me on the verge of a mental breakdown. I was viciously bothered by my "here to there" cause of conflict with the "there and want to be" reality I was facing.

I couldn't sleep (like I had previously), my appetite was curbed, and people were questioning my intentions and behavior. What was happening to me? I began to challenge my own sanity. What was happening to me? I was disputing my own mind. What was wrong with me, was I going crazy? Why could I not do what I wanted to do more than anything I'd ever hoped for or wanted? I knew where I wanted to go, so why was it so hard to get from my "here" to my desired "there"?

Consequently, in my state of mind, I began both to question and blame God. For after all, didn't God know I wanted to live for Him? Did not He Who knows all things (including the thoughts and intentions of all) also know of my desire to live a life that would bring honor and glory to His marvelous Name? Why hadn't He come to rescue me from this problematic time?

That's when the God-blaming game came about. God, Who knows everything, knew that I wanted to be a Christian exemplar in these dark and vicious times. So, why was He letting me go through this chaotic mental agony and spiritual dissolution? Was God so vehemently charged with anger against me that He would not hear my prayers and had given me over to sin and reprobation? Why was a righteous God allowing all this to happen to me when He has the power to do anything He wills? I knew where I wanted to go, I simply wanted to go from here to there, so Lord, please, show me the way!"

Satan was having a heyday with my mind at this critical intersection of my existence. That rascal had me so unsettled that I was challenging and questioning the providential wisdom of the Only Omnipotent, Omnipresent, and Omniscient God. Yes, it was crazy; however, that is exactly where I was at this particular time. I was "here" and wanted to be "there." The dilemma was that I didn't know how to get from "here" to "there"!

When I look back over my life, thinking about this tempestuous span of time, I have to stop and take time to praise the Lord. I thank Him that He did not judge me according to His righteous judgment and my pernicious thoughts. Every living being ought to express gratitude to our heavenly Father that He dissociates His holy will and righteous pronouncements against arrogant ignorance. To think I had the audacity to question and doubt the gravity of God's ways. Thank You, Holy Father, for Your amazing grace and enduring love.

Even now, as I think on those times in retrospect, I can see that God's mighty hand was leading me. I say this because, at that time of inner frustration, I was diligent in my Bible reading and study. The irony was that I was still reading in the Book of Psalms. Oh, thank You, dear God, for Your profound Word!

Today, as I focus on the rearward occurrences of those days, I am convinced of Divine intervention. I make this claim because, in looking back, I can vividly remember some of the verses that spoke out to my despicable circumstances. There is an assortment of verses that stand out, but I would like to list and call out those I remember most. I did not commit all of them to memory, but I do remember the messages they gave. They are:

Psalm 13:1 and 2, "How long wilt Thou forget me Oh Lord? Forever? How long wilt Thou hide Thy face from me? How long shall I take counsel in my soul, having sorrow in my heart daily? How long shall mine enemy be exalted over me?"

Psalm 19:7, 8, 12–14 (KJV): "The law of the Lord is perfect, converting the soul: the testimony of the Lord is sure, making wise the simple. The statutes of the Lord are right, rejoicing the heart: the commandment of the Lord is pure, enlightening the eyes. Who can understand his errors? cleanse Thou me from secret faults. Keep back Thy servant also from presumptuous sins, let them not have dominion over me: then shall I be upright, and I shall be innocent from the great transgression. Let the words of my mouth and the meditation of my heart be acceptable in Thy sight, O Lord, my strength and redeemer."

Psalm 20:6–8 (KJV): "Now know that I the Lord saveth His anointed, He will hear him from his holy heaven with the saving strength of His right hand. Some trust in chariots, some in horses, but we remember the Name of the Lord our God. They are brought down and fallen: We are risen, and stand upright."

Psalm 25:1–5 (KJV): "Unto Thee, O Lord, do I lift up my soul. O my God, I trust in Thee: let me not be ashamed, let not mine enemies triumph over me. Yea, let none that wait on thee be ashamed: let them be ashamed which transgress without a cause. Shew me Thy ways, O Lord, teach me Thy paths. Lead me in Thy truth and teach me: for Thou art the God of my salvation, on Thee do I wait all the day."

Psalm 28:1 and 2 (KJV): "Unto Thee I cry, O Lord my rock; be not silent to me: lest if Thou be silent to me, I be like them that go down to the pit. Hear the voice of my supplications, when I cry unto Thee, when I lift up my hands toward Thy holy oracle."

Psalm 85:4–7 (KJV): "Turn us, O God of salvation and cause Thine anger toward us to cease. Wilt Thou be angry with us for ever? Wilt Thou draw out Thine anger to all generations? Wilt Thou not revive us again: that Thy people may rejoice in Thee? Shew us Thy mercy, O Lord, and grant us Thy salvation."

Psalm 141:1–4 (KJV): "Lord, I cry unto Thee: make haste unto me, give ear to my voice, when I cry unto Thee. Let my prayers be set before Thee as incense, and the lifting up of my hands as the evening sacrifice. Set a watch, O Lord, before my mouth, keep the door of my lips. Incline not my heart to any evil thing, to practice wicked words with me that work iniquity: and let me not eat of their dainties."

Psalm 143:1, 2, and 8 (KJV): "Hear my prayers, O Lord, give ear to my supplications: in Thy faithfulness answer me, and in Thy righteousness. And enter not into judgment with Thy servant: for in Thy sight shall no man be justified. Cause me to hear Thy loving kindness in the morning; for in Thee do I trust: cause me to know Thy ways wherein I should walk; for I lift my soul unto Thee."

Psalm 145:17–19 (KJV): "The Lord is righteous in all His ways, and holy in all His works. The Lord is nigh unto all that call upon Him, to all that call upon Him in truth. He will fulfill the desires of them that fear Him: He also will hear their cry, and will save them."

These and other parts of the Book of Psalms gave me immediate strength in this dire time of need. However, figuratively speaking, they also brought confusion in my already distressed mental state. It all resulted in a driving chaos for me. If God hears and answers prayer, why wasn't He hearing me? For after all, I was indeed calling upon God for resolution and forgiveness, so why was God not responding by making these things go away?

It reminds me of a story of the olden western times, when wagon trains were trying to navigate to a land that could be seen but remained uninhabited, untraveled. The naked eye could view the land, but no man could find solid ground that would allow the new pilgrims to set foot on the desired area.

Many scouts had gone ahead of the wagon train to map out a route and then blaze a trail for others to follow. Some of the searchers never returned and their bodies were not found; they were considered dead. The scouts who managed to return came back with the report that there was no way to make it to the sighted real estate. The pioneers could see the land area, and from all sighted projections, it appeared to be fertile and good land.

Many travelers came, and after viewing the beauty of the desired land, would ask, "Why did you stop here when better land is in sight?"

The reply to their legitimate inquiry was always the same. "We would like to claim the land, but we can't get there from here!"

I was very much like the people in this story. I knew what I wanted, I knew what I wanted to do, I knew where I wanted to be, and I knew where I wanted to go. In my mind and heart, I desired to live a life of righteousness. I sincerely wanted to portray holiness in my everyday living and dealings. With all that was within me, I wanted to live a life in the vitality of Christendom. I really wanted to live for Jesus Christ and do His will. The problem that prevented me from attaining and accomplishing my passionate objective was not knowing how to get from "here" to "there."

God is merciful and I was able to learn from these experiences that He's there when we don't recognize it, supernaturally guiding and directing our paths. However, in all this, there was a part for me to play in seeking answers from Him. Although I had aspirations that would please God, there was a part for me to do. If I was to go from "here to there," it was up to me to seek God, not only by prayer, but also through the Word of God. It befell my lot to seek answers for direction on how to get "there from here." The answers were in the Book, the Bible, the Word of God! All that any seeker of righteousness may need to know is in His Word, it's in the Book!

I am more than convinced that the heavenly Father knows our hearts and gives us what we need at the exact time we need it. I say this in allusion to this time of indecisiveness that I was going through. I was watching a religious program one morning when the man of God on screen (I heard the voice of a man, but it was God Who spoke to me) gave me just what I needed to hear and know. He talked on Ephesians 2:13, which reads, "But now in Christ Jesus ye who sometimes were afar were made nigh by the blood of Christ."

Jesus validated this fact when He stated in John 8:31b and 32, "If you continue in My Word, then are ye My disciples indeed, and ye shall know the truth and the truth shall make you free."

If anyone seriously desires to find out what she or he is to do, the person only has to go to the Book, the Bible, God's Word, for there anyone who seeks direction can find the way—it's in the Book!

The Devil is a master at confusion and deflecting attention to what is needed by blinding a person from the truth. The master manipulator has used his trickery to throw mankind off from the beginning of humanity. Providence will allow a person to hear the Word of God being preached and taught. Satan doesn't mind these actions at all. He is, however, perturbed when the listener allows the Word of God to penetrate the mind and heart of a person to bring about change. It bothers Satan to no end! He is able to stop a person from hearing and will do all within his powers of evil to wreak havoc mentally and spiritually to hinder spiritual advancement.

Even though the Adversary wishes against it and would like to prevent it from taking place, he knows he is powerless in totally stopping it. Satan is aware of God's declaration through Apostle Paul in Romans 10:17, where it is stressed, "So then faith cometh by hearing and hearing by the Word of God." The Devil is unequivocally well-informed of this fact and knows also there is nothing he can do to permanently stop the hearing progress. Therefore, he uses his profane stratagem to throw mankind off in a mind that tells a person that it is impossible for her or him to reach holiness or get from "here to there."

With all that has been said and done, looking back, I can now see that God was answering me but I was not able to know it. God had already answered and revealed all I needed to know in His will for my life. It had been there all the time; God had supplied just what I needed to know when I needed it. The answer was right there before me. All I needed to know was right there in the Book, in the Bible, in God's Word, and it had been there all the time. Satan just had me confused and blind to the truth of it, and I was thrown off and befuddled. This was the beginning of how I came to realize that all I needed to know was in His Word in getting from "here to there."

I am grateful to God for making me aware of what is perhaps the greatest secret to all of humanity. All that we need to know in this world is in His Book—the Bible. It is not obtainable through spiritual osmosis; only when a person becomes serious and diligent through study and search from God's Word will a person find the answer(s) they seek. God will truly guide and direct you from "here to there." It is in His Word, everything that a person needs.

11
THE WAY IT WAS

The story goes that an elderly man, George, was golfing with a younger man, Jeff. As they approached the seventh hole, they came before a humongous tree. George paused, looking with head pointed upward, and asked Jeff, "Jeff, how old are you?"

"I'm thirty-three," answered the younger man.

"Tell me, would you believe me if I told you that when I was thirty-two, I hit a golf ball over that tree and I have proof that I did it?"

Looking up at the great tree, Jeff responded, "That tree, the one right there? NOOOOO WAY!"

"Well, I did, and I can prove it, that that was the way it was! I was a pretty good man when I was your age. You do know that in my times, we were made of better stuff, don't you?" asked George.

"Well, if you did it, I bet I can do it too! I'm in good shape and I can hit the ball high and far," bragged the young man.

"Talk is cheap, young man; if you think you can do it, show me. I personally don't think you can do it, you're just not made of the right stuff," taunted George.

Jeff lined up the ball on the tee at a position he thought would allow him enough room to clear the height of the tree. Jeff drew back and swung mightily—SWOOSH! The ball went high into the air but did not come close to clearing the top of the tree.

George teased, "Jeff, I told you that you couldn't do it. It takes a science and the right stamina, and I don't think you have the mental or physical capacity to do it. I'm sorry, son, I just don't think you have it in you!"

Angrily, Jeff came back, "If you did it, and I'm not sure you did, but if you did, I can do it too! Man, I have lived for the day when I could break records or at least do as well as the next man! So, if you did it, I can do it also!"

Jeff again aligned his ball on his tee with an angle that would let him fire the ball with enough forceful projection. He swung mightily—SWOOSH! The ball went even higher than the last attempt, but again, it fell well short. The young man failed this time also.

George again agitated Jeff, and with a big grin on his face said to him, "When we get back to the clubhouse, you do know that I have to tell this, don't you?"

Jeff, by now sweaty and frustrated with exhaustion, repeated his inquiry. "Are you sure you put a ball over that tree? You're not joshing me, you're not pulling my leg, are you?"

About that time, a longtime employee of the clubhouse just happened to be passing by. George, seeing the employee, said to Jeff, "Didn't I tell you I can prove that what I have said to you is true? I'm gonna prove it to you right now!"

George then called the employee over and asked him, "Will you tell this young man that I have the distinctive bragging right of having hit a golf ball over that tree?"

The man confirmed George's claim. "Young man, I can truthfully tell you that George actually hit a golf ball over that very tree, and he has never let us forget it."

George, again, with the intention of aggravating Jeff, said to him, "See, I told you. I did it, and that's the way it was!"

After hearing the confirmation from the clubhouse employee, Jeff made a positive discharge. "Well, if you did it, I can do it. I've got to try one more time. If you did it, I know I can do it!"

Jeff methodically engaged in the same setup he had done twice earlier. He placed the ball on a different angle that he felt would give him ample leverage to clear the height of the tree. He took a look at the tree with a vengeance and the endeavor to clear it. He then took a deep breath, placed the ball on the tee, and raised his body. He carefully cast his eyes on the tree and noticed its great height. In Jeff's mind, the tree seemed to have grown higher since his last try. He took another deep breath, looked up, and rocked his shoulders side to side.

Before making the swing, Jeff thought within himself, *I've got to do this! I can't let this old man outdo me. Come on, Jeff, you can do this!*

Then, with all his might in a powerful swing, Jeff made his hit on the ball. There it went—up, up, up and away! However, it was not to be. The odds were against him, and Jeff's effort once again fell well short of clearing the tree. The result was the same; the ball did not go over the tree.

Grinning stealthily, George said to Jeff, "Can't do it, can you? I knew you couldn't. I want you to know that I really did hit a golf ball over that tree when I was thirty-two years old. But, so you can sleep at night, it might help to know they had just planted it—and that's the way it was!"

Now, I truly wish I could give written testimony that from the experiences I've shared in the previous chapters, I was able to fulfill my spiritual aspirations. I really would like to report the transformation of my new life stemming from diligent study of God's Word. However, I must exercise Christian integrity and, through truth telling, "tell it like it was."

So now, as I continued with my unsettled life, I was doing well physically. However, psychologically and spiritually I was in a horrid state of disorder. My life was filled with constant vacillation between good and bad, right and wrong. I really wanted to live a concentrated life of holiness, a sanctified existence to glorify God through Jesus Christ and His teachings, but it was not so at this time.

The truth of the matter was that I was living a life of hypocrisy—a time of flip-flopping, dithering, and dilly-dallying. I was reverting to past detestable and insipid habits. I was again going to work Monday through Friday, playing dominoes in the evenings Monday through Thursday with "the boys," "clubbing" on Friday evening, preparing for my Sunday School class on Saturday, and attending church services on Sunday. If anyone notices something wrong with this picture, I have to agree with your assessment, because there is. It was a continuum of distasteful habitude for anyone who claims to be a Christian and an Ambassador for Jesus Christ.

It doesn't matter how a person labors and goes through the drudgery of concealing their sins and wrongdoings, it will eventually come to the light for all to see. No matter how discreet or diplomatic a person may be, whatever is done in the dark will be made manifest in the light. As the old people of my childhood days would say, "What goes on in the dark will come to the light." I think this was the message that Moses conveyed to Israel in Numbers 32:23 (KJV): "Behold ye have sinned against the Lord: and be sure your sin will find you out."

Well, life forced the unfeigned truth on me, qualifying me to be a testifier in telling the world that the only way not to make your transgressions public knowledge is not to commit them. Take my word for it, if you do wrong frequently enough, someone will take notice. When one really gives serious contemplation on the matter of sin, it should bring the person to one conclusion. God loves His children too much to allow her or him to eat at the Devil's table and be energized by his exuberant wiles. We ought to always remember the words of Moses, "Be sure your sins will find you out."

Here's my story, the way it was in my life and for me. I believed in God, His Son, His Church, and every Word that proceeded out of the mouth of God (the Bible). When I accepted Jesus Christ as my personal Savior, I had every intention of living a life that would honor Him, and at the same time, edify fellow believers through regular fellowship in His Church. My hope was also to draw others to the Lord by living a life in the world that would attract nonbelievers to saving grace through my Savior, Jesus Christ.

Yes, that's the way it was with me. However, the stark truth of the matter is probably a gross reversal of what I desired. Although I wanted to live a committed and sanctified life, I was a miserable failure at achieving that status. I lived a life of many ups and downs, ins and outs, ebbs and flows. The desire was truly in my heart and mind, but the executions of my passions were beyond the scope of my comprehension and staying power.

My name was ringing out in religious circles and, at the

same time, was the topic of conversation at my workplace. In my city, especially in the barber shops and beauty salons, my name seemed to be a popular entity for group talk. The most devastating thing through this whole rigmarole was that the two women I loved most (my wife and mother) were subjugated to the chatty talk. Without having to be said, I was overwhelmed and inflamed with hurt knowing these two people were pained because of me.

Then, at my job I was mean-spirited and rude. I was in no way showing a resemblance to the character of Jesus Christ. It was not that anyone did anything to me, I was just out of control. My private life was overlapping with my work environment. I began to use profanity and abusive language, and must admit, would have physically fought, if necessary. My conduct was obnoxious, discourteous, and certainly did not depict any resemblance of a Christian. Even to those I knew I had influenced for good toward Christianity and the Church, I became churlish and ill-mannered, This was my attitude toward everyone around me. May God forgive me for the hurt I may have caused to those I had drawn toward Christianity and the Church by my witness during this time of my life. This was me. This was the way it was in the life of this unprofitable servant of Jesus Christ!

So now, whether in my hometown or at my workplace, my name was a focal point of conversation. I didn't like it, but this is the way it was, and I didn't know what to do about it. I was dissimulated and confused, to say the least. Here I was again in a spiraling downspin to destruction. Here I go again, journeying into a mindset I had no desire or inclination to return to, but, like it or not, that's the way it was!

Heavily ridden and guilt-stricken by my conscience,

and knowing my life could not possibly be pleasing to God, I became increasingly discouraged and spiritually emaciated. I was right back at the place I had promised myself I would never return to. Old Satan had once again deceived me through his mastery of trickery. I was an epic example of failure and disgust, even in my own personal view and opinion. With this low self-evaluation of my righteousness in my own mind, it was easy to understand what others saw in and thought of me.

Having once again fallen from grace, I withdrew from the fellowship of the local church. How could I pretend any longer, since everyone had found out I was nothing but a hypocrite. The last Sunday I stood before my Sunday School class was nothing less than traumatic and injurious. I stood before my peers feeling unclean, unworthy, and ashamed. Guilt-ridden and rattled with wondering what was in the minds of the attendees of my Sunday School class, it was too much for me to endure. I couldn't take it any longer. I took flight by separating myself from the people I loved and things I enjoyed doing.

This time of my existence was filled with mixed and vitiated emotions. I had a gross distaste of myself and what I had become. I was angry, bitter, and contentious toward myself, loved ones, and everyone I came in contact with. And the pathetic part of it all is that I don't know who I blamed for this pent-up hostility. The only sure thing I was able to affirm was that I did not like what I had become or the place I now found myself in.

I can say, to God be the glory, that even though I was backslidden, I had not reverted so far away to have abandoned all of the good practices I had developed and left behind. Knowing this fact helped me emotionally; however, in my mind I knew, with God, there are no categories of "lesser" or "greater" sins. According to the Word of God in 1 John 5:17, "All unrighteousness is sin: and there is a sin not unto death." And it was obvious that my actions were unrighteous, putting me into the classification of "sinner." Whether I liked it or not, that's the way it was!

It had happened again. Satan had beguiled me into wrongful living. No, I did not like it, nor had it been planned, and as much as I hated to admit it or own up to it —THAT'S THE WAY IT WAS!

12
THE LIGHT

I once read a story from a publication called *The Good News*. I would like to open this chapter with this story, "They Saw The Light." It was about combat pilots over the Southwest Pacific lost in darkness. The weather was stormy and hazardous. And to add to their problems, there was a heavy fog that made visibility limited. The ground base could hear them but the crew on the crippled plane could not hear the communication from the base. All that could be done by those on the ground was listen and hope for the best.

"Do you know where we are? Pull up, you're getting too low! Can you see the field lights anywhere? I didn't think that we were this far out and should have been there by now! How much fuel do we have left? Not much, we'll have to make a force landing if we don't see some kind of sign soon!"

The team on the ground shined every available light toward the sky. Minutes and tensions became greater by the second as they watched the skies and listened for the sound of the lost plane. Then, after a long silence, with nothing said by anyone on the disabled plane, there was a sound of an excited voice. Someone shouted out, "Hey, I see a light! See over there? Don't you see it? We're saved! I see the light! Follow the light!"

The ground base crew was happy as they saw the plane following the light to make a safe landing. Everybody rejoiced because their prayers were answered.

The moral of this story is self-evident: If you or your friends are still groping blindly in the darkness of sin and disbelief, you are lost. Before it is too late, it would be wise to begin seeking the light and follow it to salvation.

The story left me strongly agreeing with the moral encouraging all to see the light of salvation. That light is and can only be seen in the Begotten of the Father, Jesus Christ. The Gospel of John 1:4, 5, and 9 connotes this truth forcefully in exposing mankind as sinners who can come to the light and be a replica of that light. The verses read, "In Him [Jesus Christ] was life; and the life was the light of men. And the light shineth in darkness and the darkness comprehended it not. . . . That [Jesus Christ] was the true light, which lighteth every man that cometh into the world."

Jesus Christ is truly the light of the world and came to the earth to show us the light to salvation. Mankind had groped in the darkness with no light to be seen. God, who loves the world so much that He gave His Only Begotten Son to the Cross that He might bring us into the marvelous light, is still wanting all to come to Him. The only way to come out of darkness is through His Son, Jesus Christ, the light of the world!

There is a factual statement that I learned while attending Bible school that intrigued me intellectually. It is a simple truth, but it carries a deep perspective that has stayed with me since I first heard it. The statement goes something like this: "Light and darkness are natural phenomena. It is impossible for both to occur in the same space spectrum simultaneously or at the same time."

At initial hearing, one may not perceive the profoundness of this simple deposition. It is such a simple assertion that it is highly possible for a reader or hearer to miss its gravity. This is true also scripturally, as suggested by the writer of the Gospel of Saint John listed in verse five cited in the previous paragraph. When the light shines in darkness, the darkness has no power whatsoever over the light. Darkness has never overpowered the light to put it out; has never absorbed it, has not appropriated it, and is unreceptive to it.

No matter how thick, broad, or powerfully devastating darkness may be, a flicker of light can dispel the domain of its murky shadow. It is paramount in saying that when light appears, darkness dissipates and goes on the run. No matter how often or how a lie is told, when the light of truth arrives, a lie must leave. People may live a life devoid of the Holy Spirit while appearing to be holy, but when the test of righteousness comes out, the façade of godliness will be made manifest.

The light of truth had encroached upon my life, revealing a shady and unscrupulous narrative. I was living a lie, I was hypocritical. I was trying to duplicate light and darkness at the same time in the same space. Now, it was all coming to light and I was being seen for what I had become. I had left the church fellowship and now felt unworthy to be called a Christian. I was not fit for teaching Sunday School. I was no longer a vessel to help those who formerly sought my advice. People in my city and at my job viewed me as a fraud—the light was on me, and I was very uncomfortable in the light!

I was lonely and felt isolated from others. Whenever I was around other believers, although no one said anything derogatory or demeaning, I felt they were judging my every action. On the other hand, when I was in the presence of people who wanted nothing to do with the Church or Christianity, it was in my mind that they were judging me to be worse than themselves. I was in the light and the light had exposed me, and I really didn't appreciate the images it projected.

I feel the need to express the "now" and "then" of the light exposure I experienced at that particular time. It was admittedly a time of horror and dread while I was going through that spiritual ordeal. However, as I look back on those times, I can praise and thank God for it all! God loves me and I am His child. I could not see it then, but since then, it has been shown to me His great love for His children. In Hebrews 12:6 (KJV), the writer declares, "For whom the Lord loveth He chasteth, and scourgeth every son who He receiveth." The Psalmist wrote in Psalm 54:12 (KJV), "Blessed is the man whom Thou chasteneth, O Lord, and teachest him out of Thy law." And additionally, Hebrews 12:11 (KJV) declares, "Now no chastening for the present seemeth to be joyous, but grievous: nevertheless afterward it yieldeth the peaceful fruit of righteousness unto them that are exercised thereby." I can now, with a voice of exuberant praise, thank God for using the chastisement of light to discipline me.

Returning to that abhorrent era, let me continue with my story. I had failed again, and like the other times, I knew what was expected of me. It would be the fourth time that I had come before First Baptist Church with the same request: "I have sinned, please forgive me!"

After bearing the brunt of unwanted conversation,

which also brought hurt to other people I love, I became somewhat reclusive. I was probably also a bit paranoid, since when I was around people, I was very uncomfortable. I felt that people were judging me or they were (or had been) talking about me when I approached them. It was a terrible time for me. I was messed up in every way!

I stopped going to church altogether and even curtailed my frequency for going out. I stayed at home, but was not really there for my family. I was just existing; going to work, coming home, going to bed—this was my daily routine for a calendar week. Every day was the same mundane activities; I didn't enjoy it necessarily, but it was my life. I purposely withdrew from my family, church, and work associates. I was becoming a "loner," which was definitely not me.

One thing I continued to do that worked in my favor was never stop reading my Bible. I read in my secluded times; I habitually read when I was not driving in my carpool (since I was not involved in conversation), and when I finished my work quota, I would go to the steel shed and read. I didn't talk to too many people and my company was the Bible, the Word of God. It may be said, and is highly possible, that I read the Bible more consistently at that time than any other time of my life. It was not an enjoyable time, but looking back, I can see it being good for me. God was working things out for my good. He was showing me the light.

I was tired, disgusted, and depressed during this appointed time. I was at a loss as to what I should do. I wasn't happy, I felt friendless, and was all alone. I was suffering mentally, and certainly my spiritual life was in shambles. I had been here before, but never to this magnitude and never to this degree of difficulty. I didn't know what to do, but I knew I had to do something, and I had to do it now!

After many agonizing days and tormenting nights of restlessness and discontentment, I was in continuous concentration concerning my situation. I had to come up with a way to regain confidence in myself and in becoming the person I desired to be for the Lord. In the words of a days-gone-by popular Black Gospel recording artist, "I'm ready to serve the Lord!" I was ready, I was encouraged from the Word of God and people who were concerned about me. Now, the only thing to do was begin a new walk with the Lord.

I had put off my return to the Lord long enough. I had to break away from the grip of procrastination, and the time to do it was now! Satan was consistently whispering to me disparaging and demeaning explanations as to why I should wait. I learned that the number-one excuse the Devil puts into the mind of mankind is to do it, but wait and do it at a later time. The adversary put into my mind such deterrents as people seeing me coming forward and saying, "Uh-oh, here we go again. How long will he stay this time before he's gone again? We've been through this so many times before, when will this coming and going cease? Why doesn't he stop playing with the Lord? He needs to make up his mind to stay or leave and stop playing games."

With all this in mind, I must admit I was in a state of stupor and delay. The Word of the Lord helped me tremendously when I was reminded of an occasion with Jesus and the impetuous Simon Peter. The preacher in me entreats me to write on this particular incident recorded in Mathew 18:21 and 22 (KJV). The verses say: "Then come

Peter to Him, and said, Lord, how oft shall my brother sin against me, and I forgive him? Till seven times? Jesus saith unto him, I say not unto thee, until seven times: but until seventy times seven."

Then, what a boost of enthusiastic encouragement to my soul I received when I read the energetic Words of Christ in Luke 17:3 and 4 (KJV): "Take heed to yourselves: If thy brother trespass against thee, rebuke him; and if he repent, forgive him. And if he trespass against thee seven times in a day, and seven times in a day turn again to thee, saying, I repent; thou shalt forgive him."

Thank you, Dear Jesus, for that spiritual, invigorating injection. For while the Devil tried to drug me with doubt, the Lord brought to my spirit healing, health, and help. The aforementioned Scriptures gave me strength to know I could boldly come back and return to the fold. The Words of Jesus did not give anyone the liberty to offend maliciously. However, He is giving all to know that if a person repents and asks for forgiveness, we have no other option but to forgive, regardless of the number of times. These verses confirmed and assured me that my return was advisable and welcomed by God, and so must it be with His Church; unconditional pardon was available. Not only was I to be accepted, but the Church must respond to my repentance with incessant and unyielding forgiveness. Yes, I have come to the Church on numerous times, and now First Baptist Church on Vine Street in Malvern ("God's Country") would have to receive and forgive me yet another time. "First Baptist, get ready! I serve notice on you, if God will allow me, I am coming. Look out, for here I come again!"

It is so wonderful to have a Savior Who receives me, and all like me, in coming to Him. He has also fixed it that not only will He forgive through love and restore us, but demands the same of His Church when a repentant sinner comes forth. The only prerequisite is that a person repents, confesses his or her sins, and then humbly and sincerely requests forgiveness. The Church does not have the benefit or privilege of keeping score, numbering the times a person can come forth asking for forgiveness. As with Jesus, the Great Head of the Church, so it must be with the Church, the Great Body of Christ! Whenever a person commits an offense, if she or he repents and asks forgiveness, pardon must be granted. It is not an option, and it is limitless!

I cannot adequately put into words the delight of spirit that welled up in my sin-sick soul from this great consolation. When one really thinks about it, it should be easy for us of like composition to understand and forgive each other. For after all, if a God of purity and all decency can tolerate our perverseness, we certainly ought to understand and forgive each other of our trespasses. Whenever, in my humanity, I find myself being stern and hard against a Brother or Sister in a fault, I am reminded of two Bible quotes. First, that of Jesus when He taught in the model prayer that we should pray, petitioning our heavenly Father to forgive us our trespasses as we forgive those who trespass against us. The second is found in Galatians 6:1 where Apostle Paul wrote, "Brethren, if a man be overtaken in a fault, ye which are spiritual, restore such a one in the spirit of meekness, considering thyself, lest thou also be tempted."

During these trying times, it was the Word of God that kept me from going insane. His written Word was my Savior! I was able to maintain my equilibrium of realization because I continued to read my Bible often every day. God's Word preserved my mind with reasoning power for each sustaining day. I did not possess perfect peace, but I nevertheless had peace. His Word allowed me to have a peace that surpasses all understanding. I found light in God's Word!

God's Word and another incident that came to pass in my life are probably the two most important components responsible for my spiritual insight and enlightenment. Along with continuing to read my Bible, this isolated incident opened my eyes to "see the light."

A man I worked with (mentioned in an earlier chapter) came out to the steel shed where I could be found when my work quota was fulfilled for the day. He was a Godly man whom God also used as an additional resource of encouragement to me during this crucial time. The man gave me sound advice, but I was unable to hear it due to my depressed state of mind. However, I saw the light through the simple action of this friend. On one particular day, my friend was driving one of the battery-operated work carts we used for going to one job to another. I was anticipating a visit from the man, but strangely, all the man did was drive up to me and say (to the best of my recollection), "You can find the Lord where you left Him!"

It probably took no more than fifteen or twenty seconds to drive up and make that simple sentence. However, time seemed to temporarily stand still. The man drove up, made the statement, and drove away; there was no conversation nor was I given a chance to respond. As quickly as he arrived, in like manner, he departed. I didn't realize it at the time, but looking back, I now know the Lord was using this man to bring me to the light.

That incident and the fact that I remained in the Word of God were the two most compelling occurrences that brought me to the light. I was convinced, convicted, and confident, and now knew what I had to do immediately. I was sorry for my sins and transgressions. I was determined to admit my misdeeds, repent, and return to my church for restitution. I was determined not to let anything or anybody prevent me from doing it. Thank God I now saw the light.

Every time I think about my past and how God brought me from darkness into the marvelous light, words from the first epistle of John always come to mind. I refer to 1 John 1:5–7 (KJV): "This then is the message we have heard of Him, and declare unto you, that God is light and in Him is no darkness at all. If we say that we have fellowship with him, and walk in darkness, we lie and do not the truth. But if we walk in the light, as He is the light, we have fellowship one with another, and the blood of Jesus Christ His Son cleanseth us from all sin." Jesus Christ is truly the light of the world and the pathway to right relationship with the Father.

I am positive that God expects us to see the light and then live a better life to His glory and for the betterment of humanity. Our God allowed me to come to the full knowledge of what I needed to know and do to be in right relationship with Him. God has shown the world the light in His Word, and whoever searches the truths of His Word will see the light! I was convinced that not complying would rightfully reap condemnation to my soul in this world now and in the eternal world to come.

13
FIGURING IT OUT

Ready to proceed to do what was right, earnestly and energetically, I made plans. It was a simple and effortless matter to achieve. After all, it was clear in my mind as to what to do, for the Bible had told me so. I had sinned, I was sorry for my sins, I was ready to confess my sins before God and my fellow man. I was ready to be forgiven and brought into good fellowship with my heavenly Father and earthly Sisters and Brothers in Jesus Christ. I saw the light and was excited to put all this behind me—to God be the glory!

There was one problem, however, that was bothersome and perplexing to my psyche. Why was I ready to do what I knew to be the right thing, and yet I had these fearful and apprehensive feelings? I'd seen the light and agreed with the Holy Spirit concerning my sins, so why all the cowering emotions invading my thoughts? There was something about all this that just was not matching my expectations in getting back on the right track.

It was also apparent that the closer to the time of commanded actions, the more anxious and troubled I became. The Devil was having a heyday with my inner cognition.

He filled my thoughts with all kinds of fearful discourse. He brought to me the failures of my past and what others would say and think of me. For after all, had I not been here many times before? Would not people remember those past times and question my sincerity now? Satan played with my mind as he presented his favorite procrastination game. He suggested that I wait a little longer to be sure so as not to face shame by coming before the church again and not be able to hold out. It was certain I would never want to have to come before the church ever again to ask for forgiveness.

Questions, seemingly out of nowhere and from all directions, flooded my mind. Why was I going through all this? Why and how had I let this happen again? Why couldn't I hold on and out? Why was my resistance so low? Why couldn't I persist in living a life of purity? What would others think and say of me? How would my church respond to my repeated repentance and coming before them again?

With these ever-present thoughts parading around my brain, I concluded that I needed to, more than anything else, be sure of myself. I decided to pray, fast, and search the Scriptures for Godly direction. I was always mindful of my past. I knew the results of my past encounters, but who was to say this time would be the same? This time I needed to be sure, I needed a plan I could work and a work I could plan. I needed, in a bad way, to figure this thing out!

I immediately gave myself to prayer and fasting. In my daily Bible reading I purposely studied the Scriptures, seeking answers that would guide me to righteousness in Christ Jesus and also give me staying power. I wanted to be sure, I wanted to be very sure, and if there was one thing I was certain of, it was that whatever I needed to know could be found in the treasury of God's Word.

One of the first things that came to my mind was, "What would Jesus do?" What greater authority could a person go to, to learn about Jesus than the Bible? The Bible tells of the nature, character, and mind of the Savior. The Bible, tersely speaking, can be translated as "His Story" of the love of God for the world. Oh, what a great and proven love it is that the Bible shows of God.

In considering the practices and customs of the Lord, I started with the Lord's confrontation with the Devil to see if I could detect any specialty for handling Satan. The Bible reports that Jesus was baptized at the Jordan River by John the Baptist. After His baptism, the Scriptures declare that out Lord was led by the Spirit into the wilderness to be tempted (tested) by the Devil. The Scriptures reveal also that Jesus had not eaten for forty days and nights.

It was at this particular time of weakness that the Devil came to Jesus. Satan will always strategically wait for opportune times of weakness before he administers his testing of God's people. It should always be remembered by all of the human race that if the Devil tempted the Lord of lords, he has no reservations about coming to human beings. It should be further noted that the Devil's favorite mode of operation is to attack his chosen victim when they're most vulnerable.

The Bible declares of this incident that the Tempter came to Jesus in His weakened state. The Master of Deception approached Jesus with three intriguing enticements. The first attempt was in appealing to His hunger. "If You are the Son of God, command that these stones be made bread."

Jesus, God in the flesh, Who could have spoken Satan

into a state of nothingness, chose to use the Word of God to combat the Adversary. The Lord responded with, "It is written, 'Man shall not live by bread alone, but by every Word that proceeds out of the mouth of God.'"

The next "attempt to tempt" (a little pun intended) took place when the Devil transferred Jesus to the Holy City and had Him stand on the pinnacle (the highest point) of the temple. This time the suggested enticement from the Devil was to use the misguided ruse of Scripture himself. He quoted to Jesus, "If You are the Son of God, throw Yourself down; for it is written, 'He will give His angels charge concerning You and on their hands will they bear You up, lest You strike Your foot on a stone.'"

Every person should be familiar with God's Word so as not to be tricked by satanic forces through duplicity and deception. We must be able not only to rightly discern the Word of Truth, but also determine when the Word of Truth is being rightly divided. The Devil is an expert in manipulation, even if it means misinterpretation of the Scripture for the sole purpose of dishonesty and guile.

But thank God for Jesus, God's Word in the flesh, Who refuted the Devil's scheme with truth. The Lord came back with the retaliation, "On the other hand, it is also written, 'You shall not put the Lord your God to the test.'"

One might think these two victorious requitals would have stayed the Devil. However, one must always be conscious of the intense persistence of the Adversary. One may win a spiritual battle over Satan, but he never gives up and we can be assured he will most definitely return, and return he will with a reprising vengeance! The Devil is truly dependable in that he never gives up and he will return no matter how many times he is defeated and/or denied. No Christian should ever let her or his guard down thinking that just because of a victory over him, the Devil will go and leave her or him alone. He may leave for a season, but rest assured, he will be back. He will return!

In this encounter, Matthew 4:8 and 9 (NASB) declares, "Again the Devil took Him to a very high mountain and showed Him all the kingdoms of this world and their glory and he [Satan] said to Him [Jesus], 'All this will I give You, if You will fall down and worship me.'"

Satan, evidently, did not know or had forgotten that he was talking to the One Who made everything, and that everything in heaven and earth belonged to Him. Especially since he wanted to use Scripture, he should have known what the Psalmist said in Psalm 24:1 (KJV), "The earth is the Lord's and the fullness thereof, the world and they that dwell therein."

Jesus, now tiring of demonic chicanery, said to the Devil, "Begone Satan! For it is written, 'You shall worship the Lord your God and serve Him only.'"

Then, on another occasion, He entered the Temple of God, and even in His anger, the Lord used Scriptures in His actions. In Matthew 21:12 and 13 (KJV), Matthew tells, "And Jesus went into the Temple of God, and cast them out that sold and bought in the temple, and overthrew the tables of the money changers and the seats of those that sold doves. And said into them 'It is written, My house shall be called the house of prayer, but ye have made it a den of thieves.'"

Having read these messages and other like examples, I considered the discipline of the greatest Person Who ever lived on the face of the earth. I concluded, and I think rightly, that my Lord used the Word of God to effectuate the nullifying and defeating of the Devil's wiles. Therefore, if Jesus used the Word of God to repress and tranquilize the Devil, how can we of clay makeup ever consider doing anything else? The power over the Devil is God's unadulterated, pure, and perfect Word!

The next question that absorbed my thoughts was of a very personal nature. Comparing what I read and studied about Jesus and His techniques to keep the Devil in check, a question was begging to be asked and answered. Obviously, I was not executing the example and power of the Lord, but what was I doing wrong and what should I have done differently? For after all the ups and downs, going forward and then falling backward, suffering shameful setbacks, it was definitely clear that what I was doing was not working. Yes, it was abundantly transparent that my way was ineffective in overcoming the strength of sin and the temptations of Satan.

After a series of careful soul-searching incidents and a lot of serious introspection on the efficiency of my faith, I was positive that changes were most definitely needed. There is a profound truth in the old cliché that says, "If you keep on doing the same things you have already been doing, you can be sure you will get the same results."

I thought on the matter long, hard, and constantly. I considered my past responses and my horrid results. I concluded with the question to myself, "What did I do on the times before when I was trying to set my life up right?" I was sure of this one thing—it was evidently wrong and did not accomplish the desired results. I was aiming but not hitting the mark. I was way off from hitting the bull's-eye! Yes, maybe it was embedded in the fact that I was not aiming at the right target, for as it is said, "If you aim at nothing, you will hit it every time!"

To answer my self-posed question, I recalled my past actions while evaluating and reviewing the consequent results. In the past I repented, confessed, and came back to my church, making restitutions that resulted in forgiveness. I previously believed that I did what was required by the Bible's mandates. I believed in the Lord Jesus Christ for pardon of my sins; I repented and confessed my sins. I did what I held true in doing for achievement in forgiveness and reconciliation to God and man. I wanted to be restored and be in right fellowship with all that was in me. So, why wasn't I able to maintain and do what I knew was right to do? These were the questions I had asked myself on many past self-interrogations that had never really been satisfied.

Then, one day in my Bible reading, 2 Corinthians 7:9 and 10 caught my attention. The Amplified Bible translates these verses, "I now rejoice, not that you were sorrowful, but that you were made sorrowful according to the will of God, in order that you might not suffer through us. For the sorrow that is according to the will of God produces a repentance without regret, leading to salvation."

After reading, studying, and meditating on these verses, I was forced to ask myself some piercing personal questions. Was I sorrowful for my sins, or was it for the fact that my sins were known and so apparent that I could not deny my transgressions? Was I sorrowful for what I had done in sinning, or was it merely sorrow because my sins were found out? Was I sorrowful for what I had done, or was I remorseful that my business was known and made public? Was I sorrowful for what I had done, or was I worried because people were talking about me?

These were some hard questions during this time, circumstances which isolated me, making it necessary that I answer them. It was also critical that I address them truthfully right now.

I must confess that I didn't like the final answers that I

gave myself. I was forced to be honest, as I could not conceal the truth from myself. For the most part and telling what God loves, the truth, I had to confess that my sorrow was primarily brought on by the fact that I HAD BEEN CAUGHT! It was a bitter pill to swallow, but thanks be to God, the truth will make you free.

The next factors that claimed my extended thoughts were, "What did I do wrong? What didn't I do that I should have done?" I had made up my mind that I did not like what I had become or what was being said about me. I knew I had to repent, fess up, and recommit my life to God. However, this time I wanted to be faithful in my service to the Lord; I wanted to endure to the end. After this return, I never wanted to have to come to God and my church in making confessions for penitence. So, what had I done wrong before?

While thinking on these things and knowing what I had to do, I was inspired to read and study the Scriptures. In my search, Romans 12:1 and 2 (KJV) spoke out to me, offering insight that proved invaluable for spiritual potency in this desperate time, and for the future. The verses read, "I beseech you therefore brethren by the mercies of God, that ye present your bodies a living sacrifice, holy, acceptable, unto God, which is your reasonable service. And be not conformed to this world: but be ye transformed by the renewal of your mind, that ye may prove what is that good, and acceptable, and perfect will of God."

I had read these verses on many occasions in times past, and had even been blessed to use them for textual support in sermons. I find it an awesome encounter with God and how He deals with His children. I marvel at the way God gives us exactly what we need at the precise time we need it. A person can read a selected passage from God's Word and discover what she or he needs as a solution and/or strength for a present dilemma. It is just what the person needs for that particular time for just that particular situation. Amazingly, this all-wise, all-powerful, all-knowing God will use the selfsame text for an entirely different predicament or present circumstance to guide His children through troubled times. The wonderment of it all lies in the fact that both cases, present and past, are answered in the Scriptures. It is precisely what the person needs at the hour of need for an answer and deliverance.

This was accurate of my experience when I read Romans 12:1 and 2. I had read these verses many times on many occasions, but this time was uniquely different. It was a new awakening to a perceived familiarity. It was as if I were reading the verses for the first time. They spoke to me with an explosive force, giving me new insight in my quest for answers. I now knew and found what I had not done that I should have done on my previous returns to the Lord and my church. Thank You, Lord, for your unsearchable riches and depths of wisdom imparted to all who seek Your ways. Our great and heavenly Father has blessed me with the answer of my seeking, and it had been there all the time and I knew it not; it was right there in the Word of God!

Praise God for His manifold blessings through the power and exposition of revelation. He had given me of His infinite wisdom, and now I felt I was at the point of figuring it out!

14
THE FOUND ANSWER

When I read Romans 12:1 and 2, I received a powerful revelation and was enlightened with new knowledge. The Lord permitted me to see all the previous mistakes of my former recursions in repentance. It was now obvious to me what I had been neglecting to do. However, now, in the Word of God, I discovered the answer that would lead me to spiritual success. What I needed to know was right there in my Bible, conspicuously in sight, but it had been hidden by my ignorance. I was now searching the Scriptures and had found the answer to strengthen me in my walk in the Lord. I'd been set free! I now knew the truth and the truth had made me free.

I discovered in these verses that I had not ascribed to, even though I had repented and come back to the Lord and my church, distancing myself from the world. It was this negligence that brought me back into conformity with the cosmic, returning to and repeating the same lifestyle and doing the same things I had declared not to do. Then, secondly, to be truthful, my mind was not renewed. I had the same mindset and appetites for life that I had always had. Truer fact, or better yet, the same intrigue gripped me, continuously dominating my thoughts.

I was aware of an internal warfare in the confines of my mind. I wanted to live a life for the Lord, but would end up functioning in the flesh. I did not like myself, especially when I had to face reality and admit my pitiful state of unrighteousness. In my mind I truly wanted to live an exemplary existence for the kingdom of God. However, the ghosts of the past kept coming forth to haunt me whenever I recalled the repeated failures that caused me the shame I associated with repentance. I had to do something to maintain and preserve stability. I didn't know what to do, but I was assured above all things that I had to do something differently.

Then, on that awesome and pronounced day, when I read Romans 12:1 and 2, I received a heavenly and blissful revelation. It was as if I were reading it for the first time, yet it had been there all the time. Yes, it was there, I just had not seen it yet. I saw in these verses the answer that would change the course of my spiritual behavior. The verse stated, "Be ye transformed by the renewing of your mind."

"That's it!" I shouted (if not aloud, certainly in my mind).

Having considered all my past repentance and confessions, I now realized my failures. I had at long last received the answer to "be steadfast, unmovable, always abounding in the work of the Lord." I praised the Lord then, as I do now, for this new enlightening revelation that He had made manifest to me. I had discovered by reading and researching the Word of God an infallible truth. These verses made it crystal clear what I should have done in my past repentances. I now knew the missing element I had failed to carry out. In being blessed with this new spiritual ammunition, I was determined to carry it out to the fullest.

In the past when attempting reconciliation with God and my church, to my credit, I actually did some things correctly. I was sincerely sorry for my sins (often in tears); I really did repent and wanted to be forgiven. I prayed to the heavenly Father and went before my church with a contrite heart. I could not deny my sins and my unrighteous acts, even though I didn't want to face the unpleasant ordeal of admission and publicly speaking out my transgressions.

I accepted a guilty verdict for my actions, and after my conscience concluded me to culpability, I did as I had always done before. I humbly prayed to God and went before my church with a petition for forgiveness. In coming forth before God and First Baptist Church and confessing my sins, I felt revived, forgiven, and accepted. After each confession, I truly felt cleansed and a sense of restored fellowship.

Now, determined to follow my new enlightenment, I accepted my past actions as an inspiration to do better. Routinely, in times past, after sinning I would fall from grace and leave the Church. Then later, after tiring of depravity, I became sorrowful for my ways and went through the process of repenting and confessing my iniquitous transgressions. I had followed this ritual so often it almost became ceremonial. I can truthfully declare the realness of my atonements. I was sincere and genuine in my pleads for forgiveness and resumption of fellowship with God and my fellow man. This time, however, at the risk of sounding repetitive, was different. I promised myself this would be the last time I would ever come back before the congregation of believers because I strayed from the Church. Yes, this time would definitely be different!

I was Godly sorry for my sins. I repented of my misdeeds, but had never been transformed . This time, however, would take on a new form; this time I would practice the art of renewing my mind. That's the lesson and newly acquired knowledge I received from Romans 12:2. I had presented myself to God and readily gave Him my reasonable service through spiritual worship. That part I had always accomplished, a task that I even found enjoyable. But this time, I was enlightened and could see my failure in remaining faithful and dependable. Here and now I could see my defect in following God's directives to the fullest. Tenacity has always been a personality trait that I've desired to achieve.

Romans 12:2 told me I am not to be conformed to this world but to be transformed by the renewing of my mind. "Renewing of the mind" leaped out at me from the pages and immediately arrested my thoughts. In all the previous times I could not remember a single time that I had ever entertained any such concept. Never had I considered such an effort that would conclude in a renewal of my mind. Oh, I had become Godly sorrowful. I repented, and I petitioned for forgiveness, but I could not remember a time when I strove for a renewal of mind.

That I might get the full meaning and impact of this powerful verse, I did an in-depth and thorough study on the word "renewal." Briefly put, I found that the Greek word for "renew" is *anakainosis* (an-ak-ah-ee-no-sis). The term describes a "renovation" or "renewal." Thusly, it came to mean "to renew qualitatively." Therefore, the word conveys the thought toward a person as in a renewing or renovation which makes a person different from what he or she was in the past. It projects the thought that even though the person or thing may be recognizable, there is something distinctly different about her, him, or it.

This information was very beneficial in making me aware of my deficiency. In all my recurring successions of failures and retributions, not one time had I ever purposely made an effort to transform myself through the renewing of my mind. I made penitence aplenty for my sins and was truly remorseful for my transgressions. I sensed forgiveness from God and man, so therefore, in the jubilation of my exoneration, perhaps in the merriment of atonement, a renewal of my mind never entered my thoughts.

With this new information fresh and burning in my brain, I was inspired to follow the directives of the Bible. I was bound this time, and with all that was in me, to do what God would command and have me do. I made up my mind to modify my thoughts and actions to bring about a new and different mind. This time, I endeavored to respond differently; I was not going to allow the world to lure me back into the web of conformity. This time would be different! This would be a new day with intense emphasis on establishing new standards for living. I vowed, with a tenacious conviction, to keep myself from being contaminated by the world. I would not allow myself to be influenced by and attracted to the throes of sinful temptations before me. I would renovate my mentality to God's way by proving by precept and example "what is that good and acceptable, and perfect will of God." I knew that all the other times, there had been no renovation and my mind had not been renewed. I had been attempting to give birth to a "new life" with the same "old mind." This time, I would do things differently because of this new disclosure from God's Word. This time, a "new creation" would emerge with a "new mind."

It was unmistakably and unambiguously visible to me what I had miserably failed to do in times past. I needed to—no, better yet, I was compelled to—accomplish a renewed mind. This time I would regenerate and strive for a recreation of what I allowed to house and rule my thoughts. I was reinvigorated with a new charge! I found the answer and it had been there all the time—in the Word of God!

After making atonement with God and confessing my sins to Him, I returned to my church family and came forth asking them for forgiveness. Ashamed and mortified, here I was at the place I had vowed never to find myself again. Nevertheless, here I was in the same predicament, doing the same thing I'd done before. Like the numerous previous times before, I was harassed and badgered by a guilt-ridden conscience, but I received warm handshakes, loving arms, and hearty words of encouragement from the congregation. Through the actions and attitudes of my church family, I felt an almost telepathic message saying to me, *We know you have done wrong, and we believe you tried to do what is right but failed. We understand that it is hard to live right and are glad you came back to start again. We love you, will be praying for you, and are here for you!*

However, the outstanding difference for this return was that I had analyzed and diagnosed my past practices and seen where I was found wanting in the balances. This time I recognized what I had failed to do. I had been Godly sorry, repented, asked for forgiveness from God and my church, all as I should have, but I had left off an important factor. After doing those things, I had felt the pardoning of my sins from a loving God and the privileged right hand of fellowship from my Sisters and Brothers in Jesus Christ.

In the past, I was so vigorously caught up in the joy of being made right with God and man that I failed to realize the need to renew my mind. Although my mind was overflowing with the euphoria of my return to the church, I now know there was never a renewing of my mind during any of my previous recurring comebacks. But this time would be different; this time my actions would be a contrast with the other times. I had found the answer, it was right there all the time, right there in the Word of God.

I've come to the conclusion that on all other occasions I was so thrilled and delighted with the reception I received, I did nothing to renew or recreate my thought process. Therefore, when the joviality of my return lessened, the Devil took advantage of me and turned my good intentions into wanton complacency. I saw myself in the story of Jesus in Matthew 12:43–45 (KJV). Matthew wrote, "When the unclean spirit is gone out of a man, he walketh through dry places, seeking rest, and findeth none. Then he saith, I will return into my house from whence I came out; and when he is come, he findeth it empty, swept, and garnished. Then goeth he and taketh with himself seven other spirits more wicked than himself, and they enter in and dwell there: and the last state of that man is worse than the first. Even so shall it be unto this wicked generation."

These verses were apropos concerning my erstwhile state of being upon my spiritual turnaround. I came back to God and my church presenting my body as a living sacrifice, holy, acceptable to God. I came back determined to give my best in reasonable service in worship and praise. I gave my heavenly Father glory and honor through purposeful, exuberant, and enthusiastic shows of spiritual worship. It was an easy thing to do since I owed the Lord so much; the least I could do was to worship Him with high acclamation of praise. Common sense should dictate to any person who realizes the goodness of God in her or his life that He is truly worthy to be praised!

Like the man in Matthew's story, I was cleansed, or at least felt the cleansing power of being forgiven (which is a glorious state within itself). I, like the man in the story, had walked in dry places, sought peace, and yet it eluded me. My mind was empty after making my confessions and coming back to the Lord and His Church. I was filled with the cleansing agent of forgiveness within. My soul experienced an emptiness of guilt, a purging from sin, and the joy of knowing my relationship with the Lord was restored and in right order.

I stop here to encourage anyone who may be reading these words and who feels a spirit of sinfulness upon them to please believe my testimony. I don't know of any greater sensation a body can experience than that of being cleansed of sin by the Holy Spirit. The sentiment is indescribable! All I can do is vigorously encourage you to come to Jesus Christ and confess your sins before Him. He has the power to give you a spiritual transfusion that will bring on new life in your mind, body, and spirit. Apostle Paul so adequately quoted this way in Romans 10:9, 10, and 13 (KJV). These verses declare, "That if thou shalt confess with thou mouth the Lord Jesus, and shalt believe in thine heart that God hath raised Him from the dead, thou shalt be saved. For with the heart man believeth unto righteousness; and with the mouth, confession is made unto salvation. For whosoever shall call upon the Name of the Lord shall be saved." Trust me on this, if you do it in faith, you too can be saved—it's true and it's all there in the Book!

I encourage you right now, if you have not accepted Jesus Christ as your personal Savior, to realize you are a sinner and Jesus died on the Cross for your sins. Please, right now, confess your sins before Him, asking for forgiveness! If you believe and accept Him by faith, you can be saved right now!

Getting back to my story, I can tell the world I was refreshed and knew I had received pardon from God and His Church. However, after looking at the verses anew, I was given a greater insight. Although I had repented, confessed, and recommitted my life back to the Lord, something still hadn't been right. In my heart and mind, I now saw the omissions and mistakes I had made.

My failure to apply my mind and actions to worthwhile ministry had proved detrimental to my spiritual progress. I thanked God and praised Him in worship (and I did so in spirit and truth); however, I had done nothing to further my mind and body by bringing in ecclesiastical activity for growth. There is an adage that says, "An idle mind is the Devil's workshop." There is much wisdom and truth in that simple maxim. When a person is renewed, revived, and regenerated by the grace of our Redeemer, Jesus Christ, she or he must fill her or his life with vital works in the Lord. If the person doesn't replete her or his life with worthwhile applications, believe me, the Devil will!

I have to be honest here. I had repented, confessed, and rededicated my life to God (through His Son, Jesus Christ) and His Church. And lest I be judged by anyone reading my words, I would say to all, as God is my witness, at each return, from the depths of my heart, I WAS FOR REAL! I WAS SINCERE! I MEANT EVERY WORD OF IT!

Now, in God's Word, my eyes were open and I was privileged to learn why I had been unable to stand and remain faithful. In all my efforts, I had satisfied the requisites for being reconciled to God. I had repented from a Godly sorrow from a contrite heart, I had confessed my sins, and I had requested forgiveness. I had given the Lord my life and body through active spiritual worship. I had been through the return process so many times I had become an old pro in carrying out this formality.

This time, however, when I returned, it was uniquely different in that now I also had a purpose. This time I would fill my life with ministry, a life commissioned to the service of God. The agonizing question filling my thoughts was, "What do I do now? What would the Lord have me do?" After all, I had been here many times before. This time had to be different. I could not go back, I was here to stay. The nagging question still rang out, "What must I do that I may show fruits of labor for the kingdom of God?"

I pondered on all that I had done prior to my return to the Lord and His Church. While giving thought on the matter with intensified scrutiny, I looked at what I may have done right and how I could improve on those actions. Then, after completing that task, I took on the assignment of discovering what I needed to do now. This was an agonizing time for me. The solution was not apparent and I found myself in a psychological perplexity. I was in a mental maze. Weeks went by and I did not feel any wiser or closer to knowing what I should do.

Then, one day I was moved to reexamine the scripture that had helped me before, specifically Matthew 12:43–45 and Romans 12:1 and 2. I was diligent in my search for an answer. I gave conscientious effort to this matter day and night. I wanted to know, and looking back on those times, it's possible that I was overly obsessed with my reckoning of this matter (only God knows for sure). However, I was constantly absorbed in discovering what I needed to do. I was determined in my search for the answer and would go as far as necessary to get to where I needed to be and do what I needed to do. I was wrestling with the angel of wisdom and knowledge and was determined not to let him go until he blessed me. I had to know!

I felt a connection with the Lord and my fellow believers, but wanted this time to be have staying power. As it was, I considered the other times I had returned and what I could do differently now to renew and keep my mind in active ministry. Acts 1:8 (KJV) came to my mind from the Words of Jesus: "But ye shall be witnesses unto Me both in Jerusalem, and in all Judea, and in Samaria, and unto the uttermost parts of the earth."

That's it, I saw it, I found the answer! I was enlightened from the inerrant Word of God. No matter what ministry a Christian does, the commonality of it all is that everyone is called upon to be a witness for Jesus. Every calling, every gift, every ministry—all is to be used to bear witness to the wonderful and powerful Name of Jesus Christ. I now realized that my shortcoming in the past had been the failure to renew my mind in witnessing and testifying to His marvelous love.

As I thought on the subject of witnessing, it dawned on me the gravity of the blessed power in the privilege of being a witness. Simply defined, witnessing is attesting to or the telling of what one knows to be true about a person, place, or thing. In considering the uncomplicated semantic context of witnessing, it is obvious that it is something anyone can do. Even if the person is incapable of quoting Scripture verbatim, she or he should be adequately equipped to tell of God's goodness in her or his life. In brief, every child of God should be able to freely tell, anywhere, anytime, anyone of the virtuous goodness of God in the care and meeting of his or her needs.

How much simpler could it be? All I needed to do was tell what I knew to be true concerning what the Lord had done for me. After all, who better to tell of what He had done for my life and the wonderful way He had kept and provided for me? My witness should be my story in telling what God had done for me and what He means to me. No one can do that better than me. I am the best witness for that privileged task!

In consideration of my past, and all my other times repenting, confessing, and returning, I now saw my shortfall. I had never renewed my mind in a ministry of change by telling others what good things the Lord had done for me. Previously, in my returns to the Lord and His Church, I was like the former lepers in Luke 17:11–19. Jesus had mercy on ten men who had the dreaded disease of leprosy, a disease considered at that time to be incurable. Anyone who was plagued with it was considered helpless and consigned to death. When He healed these men of isolation, He commanded them to "go, show yourselves to the priest." Going away to follow the Lord's instruction, they left Jesus and went to the priests. However, while they were en route, the miraculous healing power of Jesus took place and all ten men were instantly cured of this devastating disease. In the jubilation of their blessings, the Bible does not say where they went, but nine of them went elsewhere and only one came back to thank and praise the Lord for what He had done.

I thank God for this revelation that was shown me from the glorious edification of His Word. I know it is a mandate that I go back to God and His Church; it is a must.

This time, however, in my reversion to First Baptist Church on Vine Street, I would not return in the same manner as in former times. I would come back with a new mindset to create actions worthy of admission to the good graces of my church family. I was convinced that I not only needed to change my ways, but I also needed to change my ways of doing things—I had found the answer!

I learned from this incident in coming back to the Lord that I must also enter into a new commitment to His will for my life. This was something I had never seen or done before. Although I had repeatedly come before the throne of my Savior, I had never been privy to this new revelation that was now before me. Now, this time, I had been blessed to see what I had failed to realize all the other times of my returns. It was truly a case of where once I was blind, now I see. I was lost but now I am found. I'd figured it out, I'd found the answer!

15
APPLICATION

God had given me increased wisdom in knowing what I had failed to do in being reconciled to Him. I would apply this newly found information in my present return to God and His Church. I knew now what I needed to do, and that I needed to do it now.

I truly desired to do things differently. I was totally exhausted with my depraved life. I agreed with God that I had sinned and confessed my faults to Him for repentance. In my heart I felt the sanitizing effects of being pardoned through the power of the blessed Name of Jesus Christ. Thank God for His Only Begotten Son Who died for our sins, making it possible for all to achieve amnesty for our transgressions!

Here I was again, where I had been before, commencing the redemption recovery to right relationships with God and His people. I knew I was doing the right thing for the right reason, so why was I having these fearful sensations? My mind was filled with frightful wonderment in having to come before the church for restitution. It was probably due to the fact I had been there several times before, and that I knew people. People can be harsh, judgmental, and crass in their assessment and conviction against another person.

I could well understand how David felt in 2 Samuel 24:10–17. David had sinned in numbering the people of Israel, which brought displeasure in the sight of God. When David confessed to the Lord of his wrongdoing, the Lord sent the prophet Gad to him. Gad informed David that God was permitting him the choice of three punishments as penalty for sin. The options were (1) seven years of famine in the land, (2) flight from his enemies for three months, or (3) three days of pestilence in the land.

David thought carefully over the choices and gave the man of God a superb answer (in my opinion). His answer was befitting for me in dealing with the stricture before me. David said to Gad, "I am in a great strait: let me fall now in the hand of the Lord; for His mercies are great: and let me not fall into the hand of man" (2 Samuel 24:14 (KJV)).

Like David, I knew how obstinate and hard humans can be against their fellow beings. One of the misfortunes of life is that mankind can be hypocritical and judgmental against another who is caught up in a wrong. When it is another who is apprehended in sinful conduct, the "uncaught" can be quite censorious and severe toward the "caught," crying out, "Stone him (or her)!" May God be with the person who has to come before humans for examination! It is truly much more desirable to be in the hand of an angry, but loving, God than in the hands of mean human beings.

Having made my confession to the Lord, I was now accosted with the chore of coming before the scrutiny of my peers. In all of this, my past, present, and future emerged all at the same time to afflict my mental faculties. I had done this many times before and now I must repeat it again with the possibilities for my future looming in the distance. All these suppositions caused me to proceed cautiously in coming before First Baptist Church on Vine Street.

Anxiety controlled my mind. I knew what I had to do to come back on the Lord's side and His good graces. It had been made plain, and now all that was left to do was comply. I wanted to be in the marvelous graces of God and realized that acquiescence to Scripture, God's Word, was essential to accomplish this. My goal was to atone to God, return to the Church, and give Him a life of service to His glory.

This was the road I had started on and now I had to go on to see what the end would bring. However, even in the midst of being assured I was doing what was right in the eyes of God, I was consumed with worry. I could not conquer the nagging thoughts of denouncing remarks from the churchgoers and the public. I was well aware that they'd be there in abundance. When I think back on that time, there is a great possibility that I had not forgiven myself. Perhaps it was conceivable that, in the recesses of my mind, I just couldn't see how a holy God could tolerate a weak sinner like me. So, maybe also, at this time, it was possible that I couldn't forgive myself.

Yet, with all my internal turmoil and agitation, my spirit confirmed God's love for me. First John 1:9 (KJV) says, "If we confess (agree with God) our sin, He is faithful and just to forgive us of our sins, and to cleanse us from all unrighteousness."

This verse of truth gave credence to my convictions of being accepted by God. I was Godly sorry for my sins, confessed them, and asked for His forgiveness. I now also needed to make things right with my fellow man. The theology of the Bible teaches that if we are to have a congenital relation with Jehovah God of heaven, we must be in right fellowship with our fellow man here on earth. This duty of reconciliation was not an easy task. The drudgery of it was that it was infinitely easier to reconnect with God than with mankind. Knowing what is in man made it harder to come forth and confess wrongdoings. Combined with the fact that I had replicated this action many times before, I was fidgety in having to come before my church family.

Worrying about how I would be received in the realm of forgiveness, I nevertheless came forth during the Altar Call. In the Black Church, Altar Call is also referred to as an Invitation to Christian Discipleship. Either designation is an enticement to come forward to surrender to the Lordship of Jesus Christ or for special prayer. This was the premier intent for this determinate period of worship. It is an invitation for sinners, backsliders, the guilt-ridden, and the disturbed to come forth for remission of sins and/or prayer for deliverance.

I will never forget that eventful Sunday morning when I came back to First Baptist Church on Vine Street. I don't remember the month, day, or year; all I can attest to is that I came forth on a Sunday morning. In the words of an old Black hymn, "I came to Jesus just as I was, weary, worn and sad; I found in Him a resting place and He has made me glad."

Satan spoke to my mind, putting the thought of delay into operation. The suggestion appealed to my intellect, but I refused to allow any distraction to sidetrack me from coming forth that particular Sunday morning. I was disgusted with my life and my failure to live for Christ in a sanctified life. I was there with a purpose in mind and was determined not to let anyone or anything deter me from my mission.

I had come there to make things right with God and my fellow man. I had come too far to turn around, I had to go forward. I had already petitioned the Lord for absolution of my sins and felt exonerated from them. So, no matter what people may say or think about me, it didn't matter today. I had to do what I came to do, and I had to do it today—now! If First Baptist didn't forgive me of my sins, neither would my Father Who is in heaven forgive First Baptist of her sins. I had to come forth, and I had to come forth this instant. I had to put into action the application and principles of God's Word.

Rising from the pew, even though I was fearful, I came forth, confessed my faults, and pleaded for forgiveness. I was delightfully received back into the fold with the right hand of fellowship. The membership graciously and lovingly received me with forgiving spirits, loving hugs, and words of encouragement.

I had come full circle with my personal exposition and display of God's instructions to disgraced humanity in getting back into fellowship with Him. I had attentively followed God's Word to accomplish atonement with Him. I pleaded for and received pardon from God and His Church, bringing on grace in lieu of punishment for my sins. Additionally, by repentance and confession, I was delivered from a guilt-ridden conscience.

I went back to the Church with a determination never to stray again. My resolution was never again to allow myself the agony of ever having to come to God and before His Church begging for forgiveness. I say this concerning straying away or backsliding, since I know I am subject to sin. I am persuaded that we sin in one of two ways, that is, by sins of commission or by sins of omission. The sin of commission is when a person commits sins by disobeying the laws, commands, and will of God. On the other hand we can sin by omission, which is disregarding and not doing what the Lord has commanded us to do in His laws, commands, and will.

This time I was here to stay. I avowed a life of purity to God, His laws, and the way of righteousness. Satan, I serve notice on you; I stand on the authority of God's Word. I have submitted myself into the mighty hands of God. I comfortably rest on the dynamics of James 4:7 (KJV), "Submit yourselves therefore unto God. Resist the Devil and he will flee from you." Satan and evil, I declare to you this day, "I have submitted myself to God, I rebuke you in the powerful Name Jesus Christ."

Satan had witnessed all my returns to the Lord and had been successful in diverting me with subterfuge and trickery. This time would be different. I had been introduced to a better way, a greater defense in safeguarding my mind and life against the wiles of the Devil. I'd given myself totally to the absolute dominion and Lordship of Jesus Christ. Oh Satan, hear me well, as I serve notice on you. It will be different this time, I have a new and more effective strategy. I am armed with the Word of God. This time will be different! I am Godly sorry for my sins, I have repented and have made reconciliation with God and my fellow man.

God had granted me a new application of His Word, and I was under new management. I had learned and grown from my past mistakes, as well as from former exploitations and tricks of the Adversary. My mind was made up to do God's bidding. I had given Him my all—my mind, body, and soul. This time I was blessed with an even greater arsenal to fight the Devil. I would not allow the enticements of the world and the ever-presence of weak flesh to throw me off course in living for God.

I'd passed this way many times before and was familiar with its snares and pitfalls. This time I came not as a wayfarer but a warrior. I had been blessed with a new insight and had geared up for a fight! I came this time with some spiritual strengths I had never had before. The master trickster, in the past, had always been able to manipulate me and lure me from the way of truth and righteousness. Satan had not permitted me to see the profits of adhering to the messages of God. I'd repented and come back to the Lord on several occasions, as I have so often alluded to. I had also made restitution to my church and was received back into the fellowship. Satan did not mind me going through these ecclesiastical formalities as long as my actions remained duplicate of my past comebacks.

I was not going to allow myself the disgrace of another spiritual plummet. I had been apart from the ecstasy of salvation for some time and was back to experience its joy once again. I had tasted of God's Word and grace; I felt the acquittal of forgiveness once again. I had meticulously observed how to find my way back to God. I came to myself and became Godly sorrowful, very sorry unto repentance. I came to the Lord and His Church and confessed my sins. I now felt vindicated, renewed, forgiven, and exonerated of my transgressions. This time of restoration was truly different from all my other returns. This time I was introduced to an enlightenment I had never been introduced to before—I could never go back! I can't explain it, I just knew this time was different from all my other spiritual comebacks.

I suppose the best way I can express it is through the Word of God in Hebrews 6:4–6 (KJV). The Hebrews writer wrote, "For it is impossible for those who were once *enlightened* [emphasis mine], and have tasted of the heavenly gift, and were made partakers of the Holy Ghost. And have tasted the good Word of God, and the powers of the world to come. If they fall away to renew again to repentance, seeing they crucify to themselves the Son of God afresh, and put Him to open shame."

These verses spoke to my present situation and convicted me, pricking both my mind and heart. I had now been enlightened, and now, by the power of the Holy Spirit, shared in the taste of the heavenly gift. No longer could I, with this new intelligence, and also the power of the Holy Spirit, ever again fall away or deviate from the faith. I now knew that committing such an outrageous atrocity would be the same as crucifying Christ afresh by putting Him Whom I declare as Lord to open shame and public disgrace.

I could not let this happen this time; I'd been enlightened! God had blessed me with the knowledge that I must be filled with a developed and "renewed" mind in the Lord. There had to be a change, I could not please God with the same mind. I must have a renewed mind. I now realized I needed to concentrate my thoughts and actions on matters that would glorify and honor the Father through His Son, Jesus Christ.

At this point in my life I felt redeemed and forgiven, cleansed by the potency of the blood of my Savior. I actually felt free in the Lord, pardoned and exonerated from the guilt of my sins and transgressions. In my return I had a greater commitment and wanted to progress in my spiritual advancement. I felt the presence of the Holy Spirit and a closeness with Him I had never experienced before. The words of an old hymn I heard as a child stayed with me and described what I felt at this time. I could not recall the words and had to look them up. The hymn states:

I heard the voice of Jesus say,
"Behold, I freely give
The living water, thirsty one,
Stoop down and drink and live."
I came to Jesus and I drank
Of that life-giving stream,
My thirst was quenched, my soul revived,
And now I live in Him.[1]

Elated to be in good relations with God and His Church, I was now ready to go forth. I had come back, I'd returned, I was going through in Jesus! I now knew what I must do and this time I would do things differently. I'd learned more and would proceed with a new insight. I would apply a fresh application of faith and knowledge to my spiritual arsenal. In conjunction with all I had done correctly in the past, I had been shown more to achieve lasting power in the Lord. This time I would develop a strategy that included and assured the renewal of my mind to ministry. This time I would strive to fill my mind with the Word of God and be ministry-driven. I would respond differently in this return to establish a firm stability in the Lord and His ministry through His Church. I would renew my mind with the application of that which would prove the good, acceptable, and perfect will of God.

I was eager to set up a defense to fortify myself against spiritual regression in my onward pursuit of righteousness. So much was at stake to avoid letting the Lord down by living an impure life. The thought of failure to live for the Lord viciously haunted me, especially when I thought of having to come before the church again and

---

[1] Horatius Bonar, "I heard the voice of Jesus say," 1846.

say, "First Baptist, forgive me, here I am again. I have sinned, I have strayed away, again."

I did not know anything like I should have known, but one thing was sure, I was going to fill my time and mind with worthwhile spiritual activity. After all, the Lord had brought me into a new realm of wisdom and knowledge. I now knew and had learned what I should have done in my past reversions. There were some things I had done right in the eyes of the Lord according to His Word. I recognized my sin state, I repented of my sins, I confessed my sins, and I made atonement for my sins with God and His Church. However, doing these things did not permit me to leave the others undone, as Jesus indicated in Matthew 23:23.

God brought to my attention that all those things I had done were basic steps to reconciliation and recovery. However, one cannot rely on repentance and confession alone. She or he must also be diligent in applying themselves to the completion of his or her spiritual growth. Since there is no one exercise for this, the disciple of Christ is commanded to continual growth in maturation. It is as Apostle Paul so adequately expressed in Philippians 3:10–14 as quoted by the Amplified Bible Version. There, these verses read, "[For my determined purpose is] that I may know Him—that I may progressively become more deeply and intimately acquainted with Him, perceiving and recognizing and understanding [the wonders of His Person] more strongly and clearly. And that I may in the same way come to know the power overflowing from His resurrection [which it exerts over believers]; and that I may also share His sufferings as to be continually transformed [in spirit into His likeness even] to His death [in the hope]. That if possible, I may attain to the [spiritual and moral] resurrection [that lifts me] out from among the dead [even while in the body]. Not that I have attained [this ideal] or am already made perfect, but I press on to lay hold of (grasp) and make my own, that for which Christ Jesus, the Messiah, has laid hold of me and made me His Own. I do not consider, brethren that I have captured and made it my own [yet]; but one thing I do—it is my one aspiration: forgetting what lies behind and straining forward to what lies ahead, I press on toward the goal to win the [supreme and heavenly] prize which God in Christ Jesus is calling us upward."

This text allowed me to understand that although I had returned to the good graces of God through Jesus Christ, I could not rest on those laurels and be complacent. I must continue to grow spiritually, and it was also imperative that I grow mentally as well. It was a mandate that I cultivate my mind with Godly thoughts and kingdom-building here on earth—the Bible told me so! Since God's Word commanded it, I had to comply and put its application into practice with a renewed mind.

16
RENEWAL

Going forward with an expanded knowledge for warring against the Devil, I felt empowered. Now, not only had I resolved to live a holy life, but I was also going to develop and evolve with a sanctified mind. This time I would fill my mind with righteous thinking and walk in God's Spirit. My plan was to develop my thoughts with righteous thinking and actions that would please the Lord. I was filled with a zeal for ministry and a fervent drive to do God's bidding. I'd never entertained this urge before, but with all that was in me, this time I was going forward by applying the answer I had found—I would go forth with a renewed mind!

In my renewed mind, I came to realize I was "out of order" like a man in one of my most beloved stories. This man went to visit a psychiatrist. He explained to the doctor, "Doc, I've got two problems that I need help with."

"Oh," said the psychiatrist. "Tell me about them and we'll see what we can do about solving them and hopefully making you feel better."

"Well, lately I've been thinking that I'm a soda vending machine," the man went on to explain.

The doctor sat the man down and then suggested he lie down and be as comfortable as possible as they talked. The man and the psychiatrist talked back and forth in a question/answer forum for about thirty minutes, but nothing seemed to help in bringing about a solution to the man's problem.

After a long and tiring exchange that was getting nowhere, the psychiatrist jumped up, took a dollar bill out of his wallet, poked it into the man's shirt pocket, and then pushed in one of the man's buttons on his shirt. The doctor then demanded of the man, "Since you're a soda vending machine and I've put money in, give me my drink that I paid for!"

The man hung his head between his hands and sadly confessed, "That's my second problem, Doc. I'm out of order!"

Like the man in the story, I came to the conclusion that I was "out of order" and in gross need of repair. I needed to be fixed, and who could bring about a better reconditioning than God? If I was truly to be a disciple of Jesus Christ, I would need a revamped and renewed mind.

So, here I was, a spiritually new man ready to serve the Lord with all my heart, mind, and strength. I had new information that stimulated me to a new deportment. I could not respond to my atoned return to God and His Church while doing the same things I had always done. This time would be different, for after all, I was a new person in Christ Jesus. Paul expressed it best in his writing in 2 Corinthians 5:17 (KJV): "Therefore if any man be in Christ, he is a new creature: old things are passed away, behold all things are new."

A new creation, indeed, in the Lord, fixed with a new mind, ready and renewed. This time, with an intentional purpose, I would fixate my mind on matters of growth. My plan was not only to live a better and more righteous life, but to be a productive Christian. I would this time fill my mind with things and information that would propel me into positive ministry for the Lord. This ministry obligated constant concern on my part so as not to allow my mind to become barren ground for Satanic occupancy. I now realized that if I didn't suffuse my mind with worthwhile, stern, and stable substance, then Satan would. I thanked God for opening my spiritual eyes to what the Adversary can and will do with an unoccupied mind. If a person doesn't fill her or his mind with worthwhile containment, Satan has plenty of additives that he will promptly bring in.

My spiritual projection was to read and study the Scriptures, and to give myself to praying and fasting while keeping my mind on Christian ministry. I had failed on many repentance ventures, but this return would and had to be different, and my last. I had new spiritual munitions to fight the enemy of light. I would effectuate the elevation of my mind by filling it with things of the Lord to ensure constant renewal.

So, now, once again, I started anew, but this time with a renewed mind and purpose. I returned to First Baptist Church on Vine Street and came to Sunday School. I was hurt when I saw the scarcity of my age group in attendance. I was grieved largely because I remembered how the Young Adult class (that I helped in starting) had flourished and now was nonexistent. I was guilt-stricken when I wondered where the class would have been had I remained there to teach the class—only God knows! I was reminded of an old James Stewart Christmas movie, *It's a Wonderful Life*. Stewart plays the character of a man

(George) who is granted a wish by his guardian angel to never have been born. In the story, George finds out that everyone has a purpose in life and can make a difference, impacting the lives of others. The moral of the story is that we all touch the lives of others to make a distinctive impression on them.

Having repented and gone back to the church, I now had the next hurdle of going to work on Monday a "new man." When I got to my workplace, I did not announce my return to my church. We changed clothes in the shower house before and after work hours. On Mondays I would come dressed in my work clothes and just hang the clothes I would wear home in my locker. I wanted to tell my coworkers of my marvelous Sunday church experience, but could not seem to find the right time or words to express it. I was aware that I had to make it known, but how, when, or in what manner was beyond my comprehension. But God is always working for good toward those He loves and who are called to His purpose. In His loving actions, He does good and fascinating things. I was sitting on the bench in my locker aisle as my cohorts came to work. Perhaps it was my silence, or maybe it was my demeanor, but whatever caused it, it happened. One of the men in my aisle looked at me and asked, "What's going on, man? You look different today!" That simple observation was the icebreaker that opened the door for me to say what I desired to tell. The will had been there, I just didn't have the gumption, courage, or command of words to express it.

My work period on this day was a time I will never forget. I was haunted the whole day with my inability to boldly proclaim the change that had occurred in me and my life. However, I just couldn't do it! What was it that prohibited me from sharing my spiritual experience? Was I fearful of what my workmates might think of me? Was I ashamed or afraid? Would my testimony be received or accepted? All of these questions were forefront in my mind and I could not shake them. I cannot offer a reason for my deficiency; all I can attest to is that I was unable to do it.

One of the bothersome conundrums that frequented my thoughts was that I was unable to do what I needed to do. When I thought on my past witnessing acts, I came to a disturbing conclusion. As much as I hate to admit it (then and now), my witnessing has always been "by association." By that I mean my witnessing was done by the known fact that I was a regular attendee of my church's worship services. My witness was "by association" because I was consistent in Bible Study and Prayer Meetings. I was known on my job "by association" through my being seen reading my Bible in the steel shed and talking about church events with those who also attended a church. Yes, as much as I hate to admit it, I had never really verbally witnessed of my faith or the message of Jesus Christ and the Cross. It had always been "by association," merely based on the fact that I participated in church activities.

I had never purposely witnessed to anyone with the intention of winning that soul to the Lordship of Jesus Christ. It was another thorn that pricked my conscience. Furthermore, in my heart and mind, I wanted to witness to and tell others of what Jesus meant to me and of my relationship with Him. I burned with a relentless desire to tell the world the good news of the Savior of the world, Jesus Christ. I was back with a renewed mind to do things differently, so why was I having such a difficult time in doing what I knew I should be doing?

Turmoil warred within me concerning a Christian's

duty of witnessing. Such a reasonable and simple responsibility of every child of God saved by the grace of Jesus Christ Who gave His life on a Roman Cross for the sins of the world. Such an effortless, easy assignment for anyone to accomplish, so why couldn't I, or better yet, why wasn't I able to do it?

The thought of being unable to tell others about the love of Jesus was indeed troublesome to my mental equilibrium. Night and day, it was problematic to my thought process. Why couldn't I do what I was commanded to do? Was this a sign of backsliding and regression, was I losing it? I told myself this was something that I must do—I've got to do this! I must move forward! I am renewed! I have been transformed by a renewal of my mind.

Carrying this nagging and persistent nuisance around was indeed more than I could bear; I needed help. I gave myself to prayer, fasting, and continuous Bible study. I was becoming discouraged in my efforts since it appeared (at least, in my mind) that I was not progressing. Each day I prayed and told myself today would be the day when I would witness to my coworkers and tell them about my Savior, Jesus Christ. However, when I arrived at my workplace, no matter how hard I tried, I just couldn't do it. There were times when I had myself psyched up and determined to make that day the day I would tell my work associates about Jesus. I was going to try to win them over to the Lord; they needed Him in their hearts and lives. That's what was expected of me and that was what I wanted to do. This new mind made me aware of the fact that the Lord had saved me that I may bring others to His saving grace by my witnessing power.

However, in the midst of knowing all this, it proved out that I was less than an unprofitable servant since I wasn't even doing that which was an easy task to do (Luke 17:7–17). I was becoming depressed and despondent because of my helplessness to witness and tell others about His love for humanity. It is such an obtainable task that the Lord says to us that we don't really have to make a special effort, but it is "as you go" through your daily activities; that is, in your going, tell others about the Lord Jesus Christ, the Incarnate Son of God.

Although I was concerned about my incompetence in performing my Christian duty, I did nothing to improve myself in this virtue. We can all be thankful that God hears and answers prayers. Sometimes, our heavenly Father provides help in the most unsuspected ways. He is working things to our good even when we can't see it. God wants us to be all that we can be to bring honor to His mighty Name and bring the whole human race under His domain. He also wants to use the witness of believers (His Church) in Jesus Christ to advance His kingdom on earth.

God's ways are beyond man's comprehension. I was reading His Word (the Bible) when He opened my spiritual eyes to a blessing I am extremely thankful for. While casually reading the Gospel according to Matthew 6:33, the Lord blessed me in the power and influence of His Word. Matthew 6:33 (KJV) records the Words of Christ, "But seek ye first the kingdom of God and His righteousness: and all these things shall be added to you."

Now, I may be accused of taking the words of this verse out of theological context (and they may be right). However, be it as it may, my heavenly Father blessed me significantly for strength in witnessing. In this one isolated verse, and not even the whole verse, but a fragment, I received an unprecedented impartation that proved invaluable to my witnessing to others. Thank You, LORD!

Matthew 6:33 is a verse I had read many times in the course of reading the Bible. In fact, it is a verse I had committed to memory and used as a reference on many occasions. Conversely, at this reading, the Lord favored me with an interpretation that initiated in me a frontier of testifying and witnessing to the glory and power of Jesus Christ. The first four Words, "But seek ye first," jumped out at me from the page like a bolt of lightning and captivated my attention. It just seemed to leap forth and assault my reasoning facilities. That quad of words said to me spiritually, "That's it, this is what you need in renewing your mind! Take note of it and you will be blessed. Make it an application of aid in becoming a new creature with a renewed mind."

That fragment of the verse, "But seek ye first," kept echoing in my mind. Then, as I was entrenched with these four words, "first" screamed out at me for my attention and a closer inspection. As I peered intently at the word "first," I was in wonderment as to its meaning. I continued to observe this partial with intensified interest. What could be so important about the adverb "first"? Prior to this, I never knew what part of speech "first" was, but now, in my curiosity, I looked up the word in a dictionary. I wanted to find out. By now I was really inquisitive and wanted to understand the importance of it. It just wouldn't let me go.

After spending much time studying the verse and the word, I became frustrated, to say the least. What distinction was there in these four words, not even a whole sentence, just a mere fragment? Why was it so perplexing to me at this time? I wanted, no, I needed to interpret its meaning, if there was one. I wanted to hear from the Lord and not be victimized by the wiles of the Devil.

"But seek ye first." What significance is there in these four words? Why were these four common words causing such a mental havoc in my head? "But seek ye first." I couldn't see it right now, but I knew and felt in my spirit that there was a message in it for me. The notion was very strong and I wanted to know what it was I should take from it.

I wrestled in the search for the message, to try to grasp what was there for me. I laid it aside for a little while, but it kept reemerging in my thoughts. I prayed to God, petitioning for an understanding of these four standout words, "But seek ye first." It was becoming more baffling and caused a roadblock for me mentally and spiritually.

For all who may read these words and those who may inquire of me, please allow me to say boldly and forcefully, "There is a God and He does hear and answer prayers!" I knew God wanted me to be a witness for Him in both word and deed. In His own time the Lord will reveal to His children that which we desire to know, especially when it will glorify and magnify His Holy Name.

The Holy Spirit directed my attention to my witnessing methodology. In reviewing my hopeful but nonexistent witnessing habits, I was shown that one of my most devastating faults was in my presentation. In the past when I wanted to speak on behalf of the Lord, I normally failed. My witnessing efforts were usually thwarted by ineffective attempts. Even though I had a passion for and desired to verbalize what the Lord means to me and what He has done for me, my endeavors ended in ruinous, incomplete tries.

It was at this time the Holy Spirit corrected my way of doing things in the witnessing arena. He used Matthew 6:33 to show me that He must be first in all things. This means that God demands first place in our lives, in giving, in worship, and yes, even in our witnessing. In my past witnessing ventures, I tried to carry out the process by engaging in conversation that would lead to telling the person(s) about Jesus. This method was easily destroyed, since by the time I would get to the mentioning of His Name, Satan would defeat my attempt. It was in "But seek ye first" that I was shown my blunder in the renewing of my mind in God's Word. It was revealed to me that instead of displaying the Name of Jesus in the middle of my witnessing statements, I would better be served by seeking or inserting His Name first. "But seek ye first" was the premise for this objective in becoming an effective witness for my Lord. I was renewed in my mind by the Spirit of God to start my witness statements with the Name "Jesus."

That was it for me! That was the message of Matthew 6:33, "But seek ye first." I was to put His Name first in all things, including my witnessing. This was my first take from this four-word fragment—put the Lord first, call out His Name first! I learned here that when I seek Him first in all things, even to the calling out of His Name in my witnessing, He will undoubtedly reward me with power to do all things to His glory.

Now that the Lord had allowed me to renew my mind in the strength of His word, it was time to apply it to all life situations through faith. On the next work-day, I came ready to carry out what I had learned, to put it into practice. I will never forget that day, even though I don't remember what I said on my initial witnessing venture. All that I can recall about my words is that I started my sentence with "Jesus."

I was apprehensive as I began this undertaking. I was

worried how it would be received since I didn't want to be tagged as a "Jesus freak." I must deviate somewhat to (foolishly) boast of my growth in the Lord. Early on, being referred to as a "Jesus freak," "Holy roller," or even "Jesus fanatic" bothered me. At that time to be called those names perturbed me and I didn't like it the least bit. Since then I have learned to relish in such labels; I do so because it is equivalent to the time when the disciples of Jesus were derisively called "Christians" in Antioch. It was not meant to be complimentary, but it showed a relationship to the Risen Savior. Every Christian ought to glorify in being called a name in reference to the likeness of Jesus Christ. So, go ahead, call me a "Jesus freak," a "Holy roller," or a "Jesus fanatic." It's all right! These designations say to me that the caller has seen something in me that relates to the likeness of Him Whom I represent, Jesus Christ!

Getting back to my first stab at vocalizing my witnessing statements on the behalf of my Lord. I openly confess my fearfulness and faintheartedness. I vividly remember riding to work practicing what I would say, and to be sure, the first articulate word I would use would be the Name "Jesus." My mind was renewed; I had been renewed with a greater knowledge and I now knew it lay in the fact that "Jesus" must be first.

When I arrived at my workplace, I greeted everyone I came in contact with en route to my locker. Reservedly, I walked to my locker to get dressed for my workday. Other than bidding my coworkers good morning, I said nothing to no one. I just aimlessly strolled to my locker space. My heart was racing ferociously and my mind was running amok with impending distress and fear.

My conscience kept reminding me of the personal covenant I had vowed and ratified with myself. With this fact buzzing in my thoughts, coupled with the implanted instructions of my earthly father to always keep my word, I knew I had to say something in semblance of witnessing. Unfortunately, for me, at least for the present time, my mind was being renewed with past commitments. This renewal bothered me because it was something I wasn't sure I would ever be able to do.

Then, in the midst of this psychological quandary, Satan was right there to suggest an escape. That rascal immediately, quicker than right now, flung a suitable excuse to get me out of my dilemma. *I will do it, but I will do it tomorrow. Tomorrow will do as well as today, and I will have more time to get myself prepared. Putting it off one day won't make that much of a difference.* The Devil offered his most effective tool of delay while appealing to my mind. This delay seemed reasonable. However, there was another voice speaking within me. This voice brought back to my mind how I had of my own volition made the decision to witness to all of the goodness of the Lord. It was the least I could do in showing appreciation for the undeserved goodness, grace, and mercy He has shown toward me.

I knew what I had promised to do, and if I was to be faithful to my word to God, I had to commence witnessing and I had to do it now. So, while sitting on the bench in front of my locker, I had a dramatic soliloquy with me, myself, and I. I finally concluded that today was the day I was going to tell somebody about Jesus. My mind was renewed and made up—today would be the first day of my witnessing.

One of my fellow employees came into the aisle, greeted all, and then gave me a personal salutation. I don't remember the man's precise words, only that he addressed his remarks to "Billy" (and I was the only one in the aisle with that name). I felt a nudge within me to say something to the eminence of Jesus Christ. I mustered up a deep-down shaky courage and abruptly blurted out, "Jesus woke me up this morning, let me get dressed, and brought me to work."

I was pleasantly surprised with the response from the four men who were in the aisle with me. We all gave brief expressions toward God's goodness and grace. When I left the shower house going to my workstation, I went praising the Lord in my heart. I said to myself, *That was easy and not hard at all, and the guys received it real well. I was scared all this time for nothing. I'm going to do this all day!*

This was the day I learned a valuable lesson that I would carry from that moment forward. When we were finished with our workloads, we gathered at a building we called the "Goat Shed." It was a building designated for the employees to rest and recuperate from the extreme heat, exhaustion, and dehydration of our work areas (we worked in a very hot environment). It was a place where we could rest, play games, visit other parts of the plant, or be challenged via the popular card game Pitch.

Still on a spiritual high from my morning shower house experience and how easy it was to witness to others, I would also witness for my Lord in the Goat Shed. This experience brought on a lesson of inestimable value that would go with me for the rest of my lived life. There I was, with a celestial spiritual fire in my heart and courage within that pushed me forward, and I made up my mind to repeat my actions.

However, this witnessing proved not to be, and there was an unfortunate and hurtful difference. Although my courage was greater than it had been earlier that morning, fright and timidity were still present to hinder me. I was going to do it; after all, weren't these the same feelings I had when I commenced my shower house witnessing and had been pleasantly surprised by that reception? So, I nervously broke out with my "Jesus first" lead into this witnessing effort. I don't remember what followed my introductory words, but I do recall how my remarks were received. By their attitudes, facial expressions, and words, I could tell their interests were in playing cards, "high, low, four jacks, and game," and not on "Jesus" matters.

Although it hurt immensely, I left the Goat Shed and went out to the steel shed to brood over my spiritual wounds. It was there that it came to me what I read in the Book of Acts, chapter five. The Apostles had been arrested by the religious hierarchy because they were teaching and preaching in the Name of Jesus Christ. In this selfsame chapter, it is recorded in verses forty and forty-one (KJV), "And to him [Gamaliel, a doctor of the law] they [the Sanhedrin Council] agreed and called the Apostles, and beaten them, they commanded that they should not speak in the Name of Jesus, and let them go. And they departed from the presence of their council, rejoicing that they were counted worthy to suffer shame for His Name."

When I thought on these verses, I realized that all that had happened to me was a bruised ego and rejection, when these men of the Bible had been beaten. I then felt ashamed and rejoiced within for what little I had incurred. The last verse of chapter five, verse forty-two, gave me an even greater inspiration. The verse states, "And daily in the temple, and in every house they ceased not to teach and preach Jesus Christ" (KJV). I felt abashed when I thought how all I had endured was a mere rejection, while these men suffered physically for that great Name. I would be like the Apostles; I would speak, I would testify in the Name of Jesus Christ!

Also, these two diverse instances taught me a great Christian education and tutorship that will stay with me forever. I emerged from these two episodes having learned that even though I may engage myself in telling others about Jesus, not all will receive my testimony favorably. Some will be thankful for my deposition concerning my Lord, while others will prefer I say nothing at all to them about Jesus.

Evidently, this has always been the case, down through the years, toward those who witness of their faith in Jesus Christ. In the history of the Church in the Book of Acts, we can see this exemplified. In Acts 17 we find an attestation of the treatment that was typically aimed at the Apostles. In Acts 17:4 and 5 (KJV), it is written how Paul was treated while he was in Thessalonica. These verses read, "And some believed, and consorted with Paul and Silas, and of devout Greeks a great multitude, and of the chief women not a few. But the Jews which believed not, moved with envy, took unto them certain lewd fellows of the baser sort, and gathered a company, and set all the city in an uproar and assaulted the house of Jason, and sought to bring them out to the people."

However, when one reads the full account, she or he will find that when the opposition sought the men of God, the Church became proactive. It is written in Acts 17:10 and 11 (KJV), "And the brethren immediately sent away Paul and Silas by night to Berea: who coming thither went into the synagogue of the Jews. These were more noble than those in Thessalonica, in that they received the Word with all readiness of mind, and searched the Scriptures daily, whether these things were so."

It was that way then and it is that way today. When a person strives to witness or testify of the glorious Name and goodness of the Lord, she or he must be ready for one of two responses. A witness of Jesus Christ must be on the lookout to be received wholesomely or with contempt. How a person receives the witness of another person is between that person and God; there is no set reception and one's experiences will differ transversely. As Christians, we are not charged to foment compliance, but we are commanded to witness to the power and glory of God through Jesus Christ our Lord. It is a true fact concerning witnessing that when we share our testimony, some will receive it and believe while others will reject and deflect.

In all of these efforts and experiences of witnessing and putting Jesus first, it made me thankful for what I had learned. I call the "But seek ye first" verse a Godly philosophy that imposed on me a nonstop exercise. Here is my thinking: Whenever I tried to work up to a point that I would witness, I would allow the Devil to sabotage my efforts by filling my mind with fear and doubt, resulting in me not finishing my words of witness. However, if I started off my statements with "Jesus" ("But seek ye first" philosophy), it would force me into one of two options. The first alternative was to call out the Name "Jesus" and say nothing, which left me in an uncompromising and awkward position. For now, it forced me to comply with my second choice. I would either have to finish my statement or stand there looking foolish, and no one in her or his right mind wants to be viewed as incompetent. As the old saying goes, "I may be a fool, but I don't want it to be known by the world." Therefore, by beginning speaking, I found the "But seek ye first" method to also be a God philosophy. Starting my sentence with "Jesus" put me in a precarious situation, forcing me to either complete my declaration or stand there and be thought of as foolish. Then, the only next elective was to go on and finish my testimony. God sometimes puts us in unsteady situations, but even then, it is for our growth and His glory!

This is the chronicle of my witnessing tenure. I was transformed, I had my mind renewed, and I was on a mission to prove the good, and acceptable, and perfect will of God. I had miserably failed the Lord many times in many ways and on many levels. This time when I came back to the Lord in repentance, the whole composition was different. This time when I returned to the fellowship of Jesus Christ and His Church, I sensed a greater cleansing power. The contrast of this time over the other times was that I did not let my mind remain idle and in a vacuum. This time I filled my life with ministry, and truly a renewal took place.

17
ALL-INCLUSIVE

One of the commonalities that my wife, Tina, and I share is the love and desire to travel. We both have great interest in seeing all of America and as much of the world as we can. We have agreed to travel for as long as our health and finances will allow. We share an appetite for gallivanting over this big and beautiful world that our God has allowed us to occupy. We both love to roam the globe, whether by land, air, or water, and if it be the will of the Lord, we will be on the go as often, and in some instances for as long, as we can.

This aspiration was heightened by an older gentleman who encouraged us to follow our dreams. This man shared that he and his wife (who was deceased) of over fifty years had the financial means to do anything their hearts wanted to do. This elderly senior testified to me that he and his wife made two great mistakes. He proceeded to tell me of those perceived errors. The first was their failure to have children, and the second was they didn't travel and see the world. The venerable old man proclaimed that, in their old age, they had no one to care for them (physically) and they had no memories other than work, and, according to him, who wants to remember work? He went on to say that the people in his life who do for him are not doing it out of love, but for a paycheck. The mellowed old wisdom-giver made an impactful statement that has stayed with me. He told me you can have money, but if you don't use it for the enjoyment of life, you won't have any memories. He went on to tell me that "having money is good," however, according to his perspective, "having money in the bank won't create memories." This man's testimony merely reinforced that which I have often heard: "Money is a good servant, but a poor master!"

The man not only encouraged us to do everything we would like to do while our health would permit it, but he gifted us (in a very generous way) to help make our travels possible. I write this account to perhaps show others the value of carrying out your inspiration while you can. Don't put off today for tomorrow, God wants us to enjoy life to the fullest. Listen to the Words of Jesus in John 10:10b (KJV), "I come that they might have life, and that they might have it more abundantly." Then you should read Proverbs and the Book of Ecclesiastes and learn that God does not mind us partaking of the fruits of our labor as long as we give Him the glory and honor. Read it—it's in the Book! In the words of my aged friend, "Money in the bank won't create memories."

Tina and I have been on many cruises, and we enjoyed them all immensely. Our first cruise (many years ago) lasted for seven days. We had a marvelous time gliding over the ocean waters on a floating city (the ship). We ate, we swam in the pools, we ate, we walked the decks, we ate, we enjoyed live shows, and we ate. And did I say we ate, because we did eat, and good food, I might add. You could eat in the dining room, have food brought to your room, or go to the Lido Deck any time and find food and drinks. The marvel of it all was that there was no charge for the food and entertainment. When we paid for our cruise fare, all these amenities were included in the price. There were no charges for these additives; the trip covered all—the cost was all-inclusive. On the cruise, my conscience bothered me a bit for all the food I consumed in those seven days. I confessed to the ship staff as we debarked (got off) the ship, "I think I probably owe you something because I'm sure I ate more than my share." Even with all that, I am grateful that everything was prepaid and included in the price—it was all-inclusive!

Later, I gave Tina carte blanche power in our traveling plans. If we could pay for it without breaking the bank, we would do it. Tina became an immediate travel strategist in planning our itineraries. The woman became a great travel tactician and always kept a trip itinerary on hand. Two destinations she brought us on that I especially enjoyed were in Mexico (Cancún and Mazatlán). We have revisited these two Mexican resorts on multiple occasions. My reason for these two being my favorites was because of my love for steak. I have never had better, more tender steaks anywhere. Then, to make it even better, I never had to send a steak back because it was not cooked per my taste. Tina claimed I ate so many steaks that she was expecting me to "moo" at any time. I ate steak to my heart's desire and my stomach's fill without fretting about the high cost of the savored meat. The cost was already absorbed in the price of our resort—it was all-inclusive!

In these travels I came to develop a fondness for the all-inclusive philosophy. Everything needed was available and accessible for our enjoyment. We could benefit from all the conveniences that came with the cost of our purchase price. The best part was in the fact that there were no additional costs, no hidden fees, no added expenses, and no counting of our pennies to see if we could afford it. Although we tipped the servers, we were under no obligation to do so. The trip cost absorbed the price of our entire stay—it was all-inclusive!

I walked away from these all-inclusive blessings with a spiritual enlightenment. It is that way with Jehovah God Who loves us and wants to give us the fullness of His storehouse of bountifulness. Sin and the times of testing (God permitted) can separate us from these blessings. However, God wants to extend His love to all inhabitants of the earth. It is there and is always available to all who desire it. The all-inclusiveness of God's favor comes by way of His Son, Jesus Christ. That's what His Word declares.

Perhaps the thought that I'm trying to project can best be expressed in a story I once heard. It was said that there was a very wealthy man who lived in a small town. The man's wife had died and the only living relative he had was a son. The son had a disfigured face leftover from a childhood disease. The man's son was teased and called "ugly" by the other children when he went to school. The child was treated so cruelly that the father eventually took him out of the public school system and hired private tutors to teach the boy at home.

There was, however, one little boy in the town who became the rich man's son's friend and made regular visits to their home. The two boys enjoyed each other's company and played every day the sick boy's health would permit. The two boys became very close, with their friendship eventually evolving into the status of "best friends."

The rich man's son died, leaving the rich man sad, broken-hearted, and very lonely as he mourned the death

All I Need Is In God's Word

of his beloved son. A short time after the boy's death, the father died also. Having no relatives, the townspeople were curious and wondered what would become of the rich man's great possessions. Then, one day circular flyers were posted throughout the town announcing the estate sale of the rich man's property. The announcement named the place, month, day, and time of the event.

When the highly anticipated day of the event finally arrived, the whole town came out. The lawyer/auctioneer made it known that the rich man stated in his last will and testimony that his entire property and the things he left behind were to be awarded to the highest bidder.

The first item that came up for bid was a beautiful and expensive framed picture of the man's son. The gold frame alone was very valuable. All the beauty of the composed frame was marred by the image it bore. As the auctioneer held up the picture of the face of the rich man's son, murmurs could be heard in the crowd describing the picture as "ugly" and "deformed." There were also some snide remarks asking, "Who would want to bid on that thing?"

The auctioneer cried out, "What is the bid on the first item on the list, what is the bid on the picture?"

After a long pause, the waiting auctioneer wailed out again in a somewhat louder voice, "What is the bid on the picture, who will start out the bidding, what do I hear?"

Following another long silence, the waiting auctioneer called out again in a louder voice, "Who will bid on the picture, what is your bid?"

Still, as silence prevailed over the crowd, the voice of a little boy shattered the airwaves as he shouted out clamorously, "He was my best friend and I would like to buy the picture, but I don't have but two dollars and seventy-five cents."

The auctioneer carried on the bidding process as he yelled out, "I have a bid of two dollars seventy-five cents, do I hear another bid?"

There was no other bid sounded and the crowd was delighted that the young boy was making the bid so they could go on with the other items up for sale. They made remarks saying, "Get it over with, let the boy have it, no one wants to take that thing home!"

The auctioneer carried out the bidding process as he yelled out, "I have a bid of two dollars seventy-five cents, do I hear another bid? Going once! Going twice! Sold, to the young man for two dollars seventy-five cents!" He slammed the gavel to confirm the buy.

The auctioneer put the gavel into his briefcase, closed it, picked it up by the handle, and began to walk away. The crowd cried out in concert, "Wait! What are you doing? Where are you going? We want to bid on the man's luxury cars—his limousines, the motor homes, the recreational vehicles! We want to bid on his fleet of trucks and harvesting tractors! We want to bid on his farm equipment and tools! He had some purebred horses and cattle that we're interested in!" The women cried out, "Yes, and we'd like to bid on his grand home and furnishings!" Others yelled out, "We have some adjoining property that we're interested in! Come on back, where are you going? Come on back and finish your job, we came to bid on the other stuff! We're interested in the more valuable things!"

The lawyer/auctioneer went back to the podium, reopened his briefcase, and pulled out a folded piece of paper. He carefully unfolded the sheet and then gave the crowd an explanation. He shared that the rich man had left a proviso in his will concerning his properties. "I have a signed document bearing the signature of the deceased.

The document declares that whoever takes his son home, referring to the picture, that person will also take all other goods and properties, as well!"

That is the proclamation of the Gospel Message of the entire New Testament of the Bible. The Word tells us that whoever takes God's Only Begotten Son, Jesus Christ, if that person takes Him home, they will also receive love, peace, joy, forgiveness of sins, deliverance, power, and the Holy Spirit. Having Jesus is having an all-inclusive access, privilege, and favor with the Father. I think this was the sentiment expressed in 1 John 5:12 (KJV), "He that hath the Son hath life; and he that hath not the Son hath not life."

Jesus Christ, the Incarnate Word of God, came into the world to give to all who believe and receive Him the all-inclusive approval of God the Father. Our Lord, by His Own Words (and therein is where it is all found) in John 10:10, declares it most powerfully. I like the way the Amplified Bible Version translates it: "I came that they may have and enjoy life, and have it in abundance—to the full, till it overflows."

After my many committals to God and my church, I knew I had to fill my mind and life with righteousness. I came to that conclusion after reading not only the Bible, but autobiographies authored by well-known Christians. In all of the works I read, I found a plethora of convictions expressed by persuasive arguments. In my reading of and about these great figures, I came to an amazing finale. The printed words of the pages, in my opinion, all yielded to the absoluteness expressed in a rhyme I found:

> *He bore on the tree*
> *The sentence for me*
> *And now both the surety*
> *And sinners are free.*[2]

My reading showed that all these great and renowned Christians gave assent to the fact that faith in Jesus Christ catapulted them to be who they are/were. It was evident that the commonality of every testimony I was blessed to read claimed all things were of, through, by, for, and from Jesus Christ—in Him, it is all-inclusive!

My concluded conviction on the matter from all sources of my reading is that all things emanate from Jesus Christ—it is all-inclusive. I found every deposit of faith from these Godly men and women to be in total agreement with Apostle Paul's potent utterance in Romans 11:36 (KJV), "For of Him, and through Him, all things to Whom be the glory forever, Amen." It is all there, it is in the Word of God—it is all-inclusive!

---

[2] Joseph Denham Smith, "My God, I Have Found" 1869.

18
OVERPOWERING CONFUSION

Having come back to God and First Baptist Church, I was ready to commence a new conquest of life for my Lord. I was back and anxiously preparing to do God's bidding and apply those new inspirations I had been blessed to be privy to. I had made up my mind to let my light so shine that men might see my good works and glorify my Father Who is in heaven.

It took some time for me to get over my shame whenever I came into the presence of my fellow church members. It was hard for me to get over thinking that people were judging me as they remembered my past. In my mind, they were recalling all my shortcomings for censorship.

By the help of God and loved ones, I finally overcame my paranoia and apprehensions. I concluded that I was accepted by God, my church family, and close associates. And although I wanted everyone's approval, I came to the realization that would never be possible. If the world did not receive the persona of perfection, Jesus Christ, then it was certain and in order for them to condemn me.

It felt good being back to where I should be, and I was convinced I had done the right thing. I wish it were possible to articulate the emotivity going on in my mind and spirit. I experienced excitement, merriment, and I think, also, a little bit of fear. I was actually filled with joyful delight, while at the same time, there was also a sense of worry.

These emotions were generating a mounting discomfort for me. I shouldn't be like this! I had repented, confessed, and come to the Lord and my church and had been absolved of my offenses. Even though I knew Satan was present and responsible for my internal commotion, I still went through a period of spiritual unrest. The Devil tried to convince me that I was still a reprehensible and guilty person.

Wait a minute! I shouldn't be feeling like this! I'm saved and have been set free! I'm forgiven! I have been expunged of my sins through the power and blood of Jesus Christ. It is in His Word where I was told that since I have confessed my sins, He is faithful and just to cleanse me from all my unrighteousness. After all, I have been truthful to myself, God, and the body of Christ (His Church). I have admitted and confessed my sins.

I fought these sensations for some time. Although I ordered Satan to get behind me, he wouldn't stay away for long before coming back. This was another time when if I didn't believe in a real and literal Devil, his presence was never more obvious than now. I must admit that when I commanded him in the Name of Jesus Christ, the Devil did get behind me and left me alone. When I rebuked him in the mighty Name of Jesus, he was forced to retreat. However, I was perplexed by the fact that he didn't stay away long. His withdrawal was, in Bible terminology, "just for a season." And if I may be allowed to interject, it was a short-lived and laconic season. I couldn't figure out why I was in this confused and addled state of mind, especially when considering my actions of faith to get where I was. I analyzed my actions to see if there had been an omission on my part. I wanted to stay, I never wanted to have to come before the Lord and my church family again begging for forgiveness. This time I was here for the long haul. Satan, I ain't going anywhere!

Why was I feeling this slumping stupor? Wasn't there supposed to be an inflowing and onrush of peace and tranquility? After all, is it not where I read in His Word concerning peace? Did not Paul write in 1 Corinthians 14:33 (KJV), "For God is not the author of confusion, but of peace, as in all the churches of the saints"? And again, did not this same Apostle Paul write in Ephesians 2:14a, "For He [Jesus] is our peace?" If these things be so and my interpretation of them be correct, then I needed somebody to explain to me why I was in this valley of discontentment and overpowering confusion.

I get extreme elation from the words of Jeremiah 15:15–19a. There it is written, according to the New American Standard Version Bible, "Thou Who knowest, O Lord, remember, take notice of me, and take vengeance for me of my persecutors. Know that for Thy sake I endure reproach. Thy Words were found and I ate them. And Thy Words became for me a joy and the delight of my heart, for I have called upon Thy Name, O Lord of hosts. I did not sit in the circle of merrymakers, nor did I exult, Because of Thy hand upon me I sat alone, for Thou alone didst fill me with indignation. Why hast my pain been perpetual and my wound incurable, refusing to be healed? Wilt Thou indeed be to me like a deceptive stream with water that is unreliable? Therefore, thus says the Lord, 'If you return, then I will return to you.'"

Lord, I have returned and now would like to know the cause of my present short circuit. I have come to myself as the son did in the parable of the Prodigal Son in Luke 15. I repented that I may be included in the kingdom of heaven per both John the Baptist's and Jesus's instruction in Matthew 3:2 and 4:17. I have confessed my sins before the Lord and my church, while humbly pleading to be pardoned (Matthew 18:21 and 22; Luke 17:3 and 4). I believed in the Lord Jesus unto righteousness for salvation (Romans 10:9–11; Acts 2:38 and 8:22).

After completing my self-appraisal, I concluded that I had conformed to the way of Scripture in respect to obeisance. I then acknowledged that, if indeed I had done right, what or who was it causing me to feel I was in the wrong? It was then that I recognized the chief and master of confusion as the cause of my confusion and discomposure.

It had to be him, using the connivance of distraction to throw me off track. Coming to this conclusion helped me to feel joy and bliss while peace flooded my mind. I picked up on what the Devil was stealthily trying to do to extinguish the happiness I was experiencing in my heart and thoughts.

It came to me, or better yet, the Holy Spirit spoke to me concerning the matter. He told me not to let the Devil divert my attention on things that caused me to detour on the road of righteousness as he had done in the past. When the Holy Spirit spoke to my mind, it caused me to think. Early in the game, Satan had engaged me in debauchery and seduction, the same diversion he always used to entrap me and prevent me from continuing my walk in the

Lord. The Devil really has no new tricks; he just subtly and cunningly eases in on a person with a different disguise.

When I realized this fact, I said to myself, *Wait a minute! I've been here before, Satan! You have thrown this fearful mind upon me to keep me from remembering the new things the Lord has allowed me to learn. You know that if you can stall me at this point as you have done before, I will do nothing to progress in spiritual awareness in setting up a defense to fight you.*

This knowledge gave me strength to say to Satan, "No more, this will not happen this time; I can't stop here! God has blessed me with a fortified strength and security that allows me to stand!"

I was bound and determined to go forth in the Lord. Yes, the Devil had thrown into the filters of my mind the seeds of fear and doubt, bringing about confusion. But it wouldn't work this time, this time would be different! I had to comfort myself in knowing I had been shown the light, I had figured it out. I had found the answer, and now I had to apply it with a renewed mind.

In combating the Devil, I went to the Scriptures, the Word of God, the Bible, for strength. Through prayer and Bible study I emerged with power over the one who wanted to conquer my soul. The Holy Spirit warned me of neglecting to be watchful on the shenanigans and wiles of the Devil. He is a wizard at deception to make a person focus on one aspect, while at the same time working another angle to commit even greater devastation.

The Holy Spirit brought to my mind verses in the Bible that bring about a vindication to stand against the evil one. I was encouraged to be watchful in all things. The master deceiver can manipulate a person by presenting him or her things that have no merit other than distraction. He literally takes a "molehill" and makes a person view it as a "mountain." That was exactly the tactic he was trying to dispatch against me.

I was drawn to the Word of God for guidance and added strength. Matthew 26:41 (KJV) records the Words of Jesus as saying, "Watch and pray, that ye enter not into temptation: the spirit indeed is willing, but the flesh is weak." Then, in Mark 13:33, I found, "Take ye heed, watch and pray: for ye know not when the time is." Going down two verses, we find the Lord adding, "Watch ye therefore: for ye know not when the master of the house cometh, at even, or at midday, or at the cockcrowing, or in the morning." Luke quotes Jesus in Luke 21:36a and b as saying, "Watch ye therefore, and pray always, that ye may be accounted worthy to escape all these things that shall come to pass." Paul exhorts to the Ephesian elders in Acts 20:31a to "therefore watch, and remember." Apostle Peter puts his spin on it as he writes in 1 Peter 5:8 and 9, "Be sober, be vigilant; because your adversary the devil, as a roaring lion, walketh about, seeking whom he may devour: Whom resist in the faith, knowing that the same afflictions are accomplished in your brethren that are in the world."

These didactic (teaching) verses yielded instructions telling me I needed to be watchful in all things. I needed to be on guard for the Devil's deception in spiritual antics. He had already begun by affecting my reasoning power in the knowledge God had allowed me to acquire to overcome my confusion. Satan wanted me to concentrate on what I had done while forgetting the things I can and must do in pleasing God. He had me confused and rattled to the point I was almost disgusted with myself, ready to give up without recalling what I had learned in order to overcome.

Then, it came to me, or more correctly, the Holy Spirit brought to my mind the things that had confirmed me in my convictions. I had accomplished the initial fundamentals. I had become Godly sorry and repented of my sins. I had confessed my faults to God and His Church, pleading for forgiveness. I now felt atoned to my heavenly Father and earthly Brothers and Sisters.

Now that I was on the road to recovery in becoming the man and person God wanted me to be, the Devil was there to intervene with doubt and confusion. He stalled my spiritual progress with a debilitating and flimsy episode of confusion. Satan knew that if he could keep me camped out at the intersection of "confounded" and "baffled," there would be no forward progress. He also knew if he kept me there, there would be no advancing for spiritual elevation and maturation.

I had been here before and had been hindered, but this time would be different. I would not allow the Devil to obstruct me, I was determined to go on in Jesus's Name to see what the end would be. After all, this time I was equipped with a greater and more explosive ammunition. This time there would be no discouragement because I depended and relied on my own strength. I had been enlightened and had a plan to carry out the things the Lord had shown me. I was going to trust in the Lord and believe in His way for the rest of my life. The instructions of Proverbs 3:5–7 gave me the "oomph" I needed for this particular time. The verses read, "Trust in the Lord with all thine heart, and lean not to thine own understanding. In all thy ways acknowledge Him and He will direct thy path. Be not wise in thine own eyes: fear the Lord and depart from evil" (KJV). I had every intention, with everything that was within me, to adhere to His instructions. Here was what I knew now that was not an entitlement to me on my previous returns. I had, in the past, repented and confessed my sins to complete the atonement/reconciliation process. I had fulfilled the ecclesiastical mandates and was now ready to implement the knowledge revealed to me by the Holy Spirit from the Word of God. I'd been here before and had been hindered by the Devil's cunningly devised distractions. However, Satan, I would like to serve notice on you in letting you know this comeback will be handled differently. I will come back with a new mindset. I've come back transformed, my body is a present to God as a living sacrifice. I refuse to allow the Devil or the enticement of the world to bring me into conformity—I'm changed! There is a new mind in me, it has been renewed with Godly knowledge and wisdom. The Holy Spirit has blessed me with enlightenment of additional information. This time I see more clearly, I have seen the light, and I will operate under the power and authority of Jesus Christ.

It may seem strange since I can't find the words to articulate the feelings housed within me at this time. It may appear strange to some when they read my next statement. I was what you may consider abnormal, but I was, in an odd sort of way, excited to function in accord with God's Word and Spirit in my upcoming battle with the Devil. I felt this way because I was thrilled as I felt the loosening of my mind from the Satanic afflictions that had me bound.

Admittedly, temporarily, at least, I was in the grips of confusion. Satan had my mind. However, when the Holy Spirit activated His power to bring back to my memory the things of God, I revived. From God's Word I was able, by my faith actions, to order the Devil, in the Name of Jesus Christ, to "Begone!" It was successful and my confusion disappeared, leaving a calm serenity. Thank You, heavenly Father, for the power of Your Word. It allowed me to overpower the Devil's confusion and chase it away.

19
THE END RESULTS

Time transported me into the present day. I was still glorifying the Lord while striving to do His will. There was a daily hunger in me to know more about God and grow in his Word. I was filled with an insatiable passion and desire to search the Scriptures for personal growth. Although I was misinterpreted and accused of wanting to be a grandstander who only wanted to flaunt my knowledge, it could not have been further from the truth. I truly did, admittedly, want my Bible cognition to be noticed, but my greatest desire was for a more noble reason. I wanted to share and distribute my Bible scholarship for the growth of others for advancement in the Word of God (God as my witness!). What others said and thought of me may have maimed me had I not known in my own mind that their unfair and unjust judgments were inaccurate. I was assured by a clear conscience of the purity and righteousness of my intentions.

I settled down to a life of satisfaction and contentment in becoming a better husband and father figure. My family life had greatly improved as my children were growing up and becoming interested in sporting and church events.

My domino playing with "the boys" was now substituted with family games. We had accumulated a hefty stack of board games to satisfy our competitive spirits. We began to make bowling a family sport outing since it was affordable. I could actually take my family of five to the bowling alley for an evening of fun for about twenty-five dollars without overly straining our budget.

At this point in my life, I was not frequenting the local hangout clubs where I "shot dice" in gambling feats. Not that I was losing at the crap table (or floor), but I was convicted in my studying of God's Word that it was wrong. It was apparent, as well, that by staying home with my family, other vices, ungodly acts, and grace errors (sin) were greatly curtailed.

It was a better time for me in every aspect of my life. Satan was still present to offer seductive temptations, but I was always successful in resisting the onslaughts. I was vigilant by keeping myself prepared to rebuke the master trickster with the Word of God. If there was one thing I had learned in my spiritual development it was that I am a disciple (follower/learner) of Jesus Christ. When I examine and study the life of Jesus in the Gospels, it surely displays the fact that even He, the Incarnate Son of God, was not exempt from the villainy and depraved allurements of the Devil. The gleaning I gathered from this purview of information is how Jesus responded to the Evil One.

When I considered afresh Jesus's methodology of dealing with the Prince of Darkness, I determined in my mind that if it was good enough for Jesus, it surely was good enough for me! I made a personal commitment that I would always stay in the Word of God. It made it easier for the Holy Spirit to function in His promised role. Jesus said this of the perfunctory assignment to believers in John

14:26 (KJV), "But the Comforter, which is the Holy Ghost Whom the Father will send in My Name, He will teach you all things and bring all things to your remembrance, whatsoever I have said to you."

The Lord declared that He (the Holy Spirit) will teach you in all things. There are four ways the Holy Spirit imparts knowledge to humans. He speaks directly to hearts, He reveals through chosen vessels (people), He divulges through dreams and visions, and He also shows the way through His Holy Written Word.

As people, especially we who are Christians, we are obligated to receive and hold fast to the Word of God. Jesus stated that one of the functions of the Holy Spirit is to bring all things to our remembrance. Therefore, it would behoove all to read, study, and commit to memory the teachings (Word) of God. As potent as the omnipotent power of the Holy Spirit is, it is impossible for even Him to bring to something that has not been transmitted to us for learning purposes. To be blessed to the fullest, a person has to study; it is not automatic just because we are Christians. There is no spiritual osmosis.

We should be familiar with God's Word to know what He expects of us in our relationship to the heavenly Father (Creator) and fellow man (humanity). The Scriptures inform that mankind can only conquer the issue of ignorance toward God via His Word. When we know better, our heavenly Father expects us to do better. Paul expressed it appropriately when he preached to the people at Mars Hill. As stated in Acts 17:30 (KJV), "And the times of this ignorance God winked at, but now commendeth all men every where to repent."

Reading Scriptures daily had become a constant habit that I relished. I would get up early enough before going to work for a time of reading and prayer. When I was not driving in our carpool, I read my Bible or some other religious material. Daily, after completing my work quota, most generally I could be found in the steel shed reading my Bible. No one could rightly fault me for not reading my Bible. On the way home, when I was not driving, my daily ride time was spent reading. I had become an avid reading academician and thoroughly enjoyed it. I was strengthening myself to wage war against Satan, and at the same time, put myself in a spiritual position for enabling the Holy Spirit in reminding power for growth.

God blessed me in being able to navigate and advance my spiritual ecumenical matters. My mind was undergoing renovations for the emergence of spiritual maturation. I was purposely making sure my mind was fed on God's Word. Even though I was perceived and condemned by some to be conceited and pompous, I knew in my heart and mind that was not the case. My mind was suffused with Scriptures and in the Words of Jesus as recorded in Matthew 12:34 and Luke 6:45 (using Luke's quote), "A good man out of the good treasures of his heart bringeth forth that which is good; and an evil man out of the evil treasures of his heart that which is evil: for out of the abundance of the heart his mouth speaketh" (KJV). All I was doing was speaking out of the content abundance of my mind. I was like a little boy who for the first time observes himself in the mirror. He is enthused and fascinated with the synchronized movement of his likeness in the reflection. After a few moments of stimulated movements and making faces, the impressionable child blurts out to his mother, "Mommy, that's me!"

It also helped me to note that mankind has never been complimentary toward those who want to grow in the

Lord and carry out His Word through exemplary living. Knowing this lifted my spirits to encourage me to read more and to glorify the fact that I was able to suffer in the same way as did Godly servants of olden days and the present.

God was blessing every area of my life. My spiritual affairs were in order as I was expanding in the work and knowledge of the Lord. I was leading my family, performing the priestly duties as a father by demanding respect for God and His house (the Church). I was like Joshua when he declares in Joshua 24:15 (New American Standard Version), "And if it is disagreeable in your sight to serve the Lord, choose for yourselves today whom you will serve: Whether the gods which your fathers served which were beyond the River, or the gods of the Amorites in whose land you are living, but as for me and my house, we will serve the Lord." This was also my conviction and the rule for everyone under the roof of my house.

I continued to witness to others using the "Jesus first" formula I had learned from the Lord through inspiration of Scripture (God's Word). Coworkers and friends had regained enough confidence in me to ask me for my advice and counsel. I was blessed with much-needed overtime to supplement our family income. Everything was going well for me—a happy wife (as the saying goes, "happy wife, happy life"), healthy and behaved children (we received compliments on their behavior by teachers and even strangers in public), satisfactory finances—we were definitely experiencing the favor of the Lord!

Lest any should conclude from my testimony that all things were unerring, that I was living a life filled with a bed of roses, let me be quick to set the record straight. Although things overall were going well for my family and me, there were some contentions we had to deal with. My wife and I, like most married couples, had our disagreements; our children were not perfect and committed punishable actions; unforeseen repairs cropped up; and sometimes we were strained financially. Our advantage was in the fact that our confidence was in God, through, by, and in His Word.

It may be boring to read, but I'd like to stop here and list several verses that gave (and still give) me inspiration in troubled times. I have come to the conclusion that trust in God (faith) is the solution to all arduous circumstances in life. God is, as Apostle Paul coins in Ephesians 3:20 (KJV), "Able to do exceeding abundantly above all that we ask or think, according to the power [which I believe to be faith] that worketh in us." If a person can believe it, and if it be the will of God, all things are possible. Another way of putting it is, "If a person has the faith, God has the power!"

Here are the verses that gave me solace and consolation, which I hope will bless also all who read them:

Job 13:15a (KJV): "Though He slay me, yet will I trust in Him."

Psalm 25:2 and 3 (AMP): "Oh my God, I trust, lean on, rely on and am confident in You; let me not be put to shame or [hope in You] be disappointed; let them be ashamed who forsake the right or deal treacherously without cause."

Psalm 37:3 (KJV): "Trust in the Lord, and do good; so shalt thou dwell in the land and verily thou shalt be fed."

Psalm 55:22 and 23 (AMP): "Cast your burdens on the Lord [releasing the weight of it] and He will sustain you; He will never allow the consistently righteous to be moved—made to slip, fall, or fail. But You, O God, will bring down the wicked to the pit of destruction; men of blood and treachery shall not live out half their days; but I will trust, lean on and confidently rely on You."

Psalm 56:3 and 4 (NIV): "When I am afraid, I will trust in You. In God Whose Word I praise, in God I trust; I will not be afraid. What can mortal man do to me?"

Psalm 118:8 (AMP): "It is better to trust and take refuge in the Lord than to put confidence in man."

Psalm 143:8 (KJV): "Cause me to hear Thy loving kindness in the morning; for in Thee do I trust: cause me to know the way wherein I should walk, for I lift up my soul into Thee."

Psalm 144:2 (AMP): "My steadfast love and my fortress, my high tower and my deliverer, my shield and He in Whom I trust and take refuge, Who subdues my people under me."

These and other like verses (that I didn't list), I constantly read and committed to memory. These and the other verses served well in providing me strength during intense times of Satanic assaults. Whenever the Devil mounted an attack against me, I learned not to trust in my own might. I became convinced (and remain so today) that no matter what I attempted to do or say of myself, it was all in vain. The end result of all self-righteousness and cockiness is failure. The only way to overcome Satan's invasion is to arm the mind with the Word of God. He can't stand against it!

I achieved spiritual victory whenever I applied God's Word as a defense. It felt good to know and see I could put the Devil to flight with Scripture. I learned from the Master, the superlative of heaven and earth, how to keep the Adversary defeated and powerless. In spite of human efforts and execution, the thrill of victory against the Devil can only be accomplished by and through the Word of God. No human being can bring about the agony of defeat to Satan by any fleshly means. Success is procured exclusively by and through the might of God's Word—it's the end result!

Now, with all this in witnessing to the power and might of the Holy Spirit, there is an admission I must confess to. I was content and satisfied in my home life as a husband and father. I enjoyed my family time of playing games and going bowling. I was faithful in attending church and worship. I was reading and studying my Bible with ardent passion, growing in knowledge and wisdom. I was also supplementing my Scripture reading with exegesis and explanatory commentary from renowned and learned Bible scholars. The end result was that I was growing in Word and deed (no bragging, just facts!).

However, and in keeping with the integrity of truth, with all these notable and measurable outcomes, I still experienced inner turmoil. Although uninvited, unwanted temptations encroached my mind. When I least suspected it, unsavory thoughts and evil tendencies would arouse my basest desires. Memories of past activities rushed forth to bring disturbances to my mind. These were feelings and emotions I thought long gone and were just regrets of the past. The end result was, however, that they were gone from the mind but not forgotten in the flesh.

Concerned and somewhat fearful, I fretted about my destiny. I wondered if this was déjà vu, that I was going through what I had experienced before. Was this the verge of a decline in doing what I said I would never do again? Challenged yet again with the quagmire of duplicity—realness and hypocrisy, right and wrong, good and evil—I was once again brought face to face with bewilderment. I wanted to continue my walk in the Lord, but there was, at one and the same time, a diabolical lusting in the flesh.

Perplexed and afraid, I was moved to prayer and fasting. I couldn't go back. I recalled the Words of Jesus to His disciples after they were unable to heal a demon-possessed young man. When the disciples asked of their inability to cast out the demon, He said to them, "Howbeit, this kind goeth out but by prayer and fasting" (Matthew 17:21 (KJV)). This may have been one of those "this kind" of situations and I needed the Lord's power and intervention.

God heard my prayers and honored my supplication of prayer and fasting. The Holy Spirit brought to my memory the unfinished things I had declared to do in my return to the Lord and my church.

Although I had done many things in proper fashion and application, it came to me that I had left off a component I had decreed to assure permanency in my recommitment to my Lord and Savior, Jesus Christ. I truly had repented, confessed my sins, and received forgiveness from God and from His Church. I had ardently and relentlessly read and studied the Holy Writ (the Bible). I was keeping with Biblical mandates in reconciled atonement with God and my fellow man. However, through the prompting of the Holy Spirit I became aware of my shortcoming in failing to do the things I had vowed to do. The Spirit brought back to my memory what I had learned from the story of the man whose end result was worse at the last than it was at the first status. I was successful in filling my mind with spiritual information, but there was yet a void, and Satan was doing all in his power to fill it. It is true that I had renewed and filled my mind with Biblical data, but I was tolerating idleness of my hands. I had earlier made covenant with myself that I would engage my earthly existence to include worthwhile ministry in service to the honor of Christ Jesus. Thank You, Holy Spirit, for bringing it to my remembrance; I had forgotten to include a promised involvement in ministry when I returned to the Lord and my church.

So now, with this remembrance strong on my mind, the need to include ministry in my life must be *sine qua non* (something absolutely essential). I prayed to God for direction in following His will for my life. My question to my heavenly Father was concise and direct: "Lord, what would You have me to do?" I now know I had to apply my hands to beneficial ministry in God's vineyard (earth). Then, in the Word of God, I read from Paul's letter to the Romans 12:6–8 (KJV), "Having then gifts differing according to the grace given to us, whether prophesy, let us prophesy according to the proportion of faith; Or ministry, let us wait on our ministering: or he that teacheth on teaching; Or he that exhorted, on exhortation: he that giveth, let him do it with simplicity, he that ruleth, with diligence; he that sheweth mercy, with cheerfulness."

With these verses on my brain, the fourth chapter of the Book of Acts, verses thirty-six and thirty-seven, also claimed my attention. These verses, from the New International Version, read, "Joseph, a Levite from Cyprus, whom the apostles called Barnabus [which means Son of Encouragement], sold a field and brought the money and put it at the apostle's feet." This Barnabus (Son of Encouragement) stood out to me and sharpened my interest concerning his personality. In studying his disposition in the Book of Acts, I saw him portrayed as a man who rallied in favor of another (the underdog, my description). Acts records two notable incidents when

Barnabus stood in the gap for someone: he stood up before the church on behalf of Paul (then known as notorious Saul), and also in the support of his nephew, John Mark.

From reading about the character of Barnabus (which I read in God's Word), I instinctively knew this was a characteristic I wanted to emulate. I remembered reading once that God often matches the calling upon our lives with gifts to coincide with our personalities. This was particularly true in my case since I am a person who always roots for the underdog and wants to see people succeed. This was my answer, and I found it in God's Word, the Bible, the answer to the world's problems. I immediately recognized the call upon my life to be an encourager. This was my calling, this was the ministry I felt led to undertake to the glory of my Lord and Savior, Jesus Christ. I would devote my life to raising other people's confidence in themselves, in others, and most of all, in God. When someone was dispirited or disheartened, I would embolden them with words of encouragement. This was my calling, this was my ministry, this was what I would do to the glory of God—the end result of my ministry was to be an encourager.

Since I have committed to becoming an encourager, I hope those I have helped have been as blessed by this ministry as I have been. It has been exhilarating to see people express emotional stimulation because of something I have said or done for them. I have been blessed to be the recipient of acclaim by young and old, male and female, because I fulfilled my calling in the ministry of encouragement. It has truly been a seal of approval, at least in my mind, of my gift in ministry. I had already been encouraging people, but did not realize it as a ministry until I found it in the Word of God!

I was ready to close this chapter when a story entitled the same as this chapter, "End Result," came to my mind. This story (an original) came to me some years ago. I don't know whether it's relevant, but since it came to my mind here goes:

A man walked down the sidewalk on a hot and sulky day when he came upon a welcome sight. A little boy was sitting behind a table under a patio umbrella with a handwritten sign that read, "END RESULT, ALL YOU CAN DRINK—25 CENTS."

On the table was a big jug of lemonade filled with ice cubes. The day was hot and the lemonade looked appetizing as condensation ran down the outside of the jug. The man, wanting to help the young boy out and at the same time wet his parched throat, gave the boy a quarter and was given a cup of the brew. He gulped the drink down and after finishing it, sat the glass on the table. The man said to the boy, "Say! That's pretty good. I think I'll have another glassful!"

To the man's surprise, the boy reached out his hand and declared, "That'll be twenty-five cents, please!"

"Twenty-five cents," said the man. "But your sign says, 'END RESULT, ALL YOU CAN DRINK—25 CENTS'!"

"Yes, sir, you read the sign right," the little boy answered back. "The end result is that one glass is ALL YOU CAN DRINK for twenty-five cents!"

20
GETTING IT

It is a universal truth that no one is perfect and without flaw. Any person born of the fruit of the womb is innately morally reprehensible. An unfortunate quality of human DNA composition is its propensity to sin and error. The nature of sin in humans evolves from the progenitors of humanity, Adam and Eve. We, all of fleshly makeup, are surfeited with the Word of God, "There is none good, no not one."

In a conversation with a Brother (in the Lord), I was flabbergasted by what I believed (and still do today) to be downright outlandish. He made the statement that he doesn't sin. Even after I gave him opportunity to retract such a ridiculous claim, he held firm to his declaration. I honestly hoped he had possibly made a slip of the tongue. However, he held strong to his profession and was adamant in what he had said.

After a brief debate on the subject matter and following a few moments of silence, I spoke out. My reply to hm was, "Congratulations, my Brother! You've just joined the human race!"

Puzzled, and perhaps startled by my remark, the man

looked at me with an inquisitive expression. He asked, "What do you mean by that?"

After getting his permission to be completely honest with him, I proceeded to tell him the truth as I saw it. I replied, "Well, the way I see it, if you have never sinned to this point, you have just joined the rest of the human race."

There was a long pause, and the look on his face suggested that I needed to make further clarification. I went on to tell him, "With that lie, you've just joined the human race and the rest of world, because with what you just told me, you've just started sinning since lying is a sin."

I was doing all I could do to propel my life into living for the Lord. I was growing in the Word of God, developing an addiction for spiritual comprehension. I was maturing in Scripture attainment and delighted in sharing my learning with others. My witnessing to people had blossomed and developed into a regular frequency. I was faithful in my church attendance and affiliation to the degree that when I was not present, my fellow worshipers would be concerned about my well-being. I felt the power of the Holy Spirit Who brought me to higher heights in spiritual maturation.

Now, lest someone read more into my words than I am saying and my testimony be misconstrued, I think it prudent for me to offer further details. At this point in my life, I had received an increase in my family size, finances, and religiosity. Things were going well for me physically, mentally, and spiritually.

This does not mean my life was perfect, in fact it was the opposite. My life was not devoid of problems. It was nowhere near perfection, although I strove for it, as I feel should be the endeavor of every child of God. My stance in life could correspond with Paul's disclosure in Philippians

4:8–14. It was not that I had reached perfection in my knowledge of God or living without sin. Although perfection was my ideal and my objective, I was far from attaining it.

Through the years I had been accosted and victimized by addiction to nicotine. The habit captivated my taste buds gradually. I started smoking to "fit in," to "be cool," if you will, with the people I fraternized with. When I started smoking, I was able to quit and start at will. I even boasted of my ability to discontinue my tobacco habit whenever I chose.

My flamboyant bragging was true for quite some time. I would smoke for a while and then lay the cigarettes aside and not use them. In my mind I was in complete control of my body and taste. I was successful in overcoming naysayers who were skeptical of my claim. To prove my assertion right and my dissenters wrong, I would stop using tobacco for a specified time. The stoppage was often accompanied by a wager since the other person felt that because he was addicted, I was also. It was an easy taking and I was rewarded for my resistance. I smoked, but I was able to start and quit at will—I was not addicted.

However, as time went on and I continued to smoke, I lost my mastery over my tobacco habit. The day came when my body craved nicotine. The more I struggled against the yearning for tobacco, the greater the dependence became. The master had become the slave, the hunter was now the game. I came to the realization that I was addicted.

Now, a few years later, married with children, and a professed "grown man," I was a full-fledged smoker. I had given in to the seduction and admitted to enjoying cigarette smoking. I bought a carton (ten-pack) of cigarettes a week. In the past I was an occasional smoker, but now I was a habitual user. My breath was contaminated with the odor of tobacco and my clothes reeked with its repugnant stench. I have witnessed many debates on the subject of smoking, both for and against, pro and con. I heard a preacher once proclaim, "I don't know if smoking will send a person to hell or not, but it does make the person smell like she or he has been there."

I am convinced that smoking harms the body (the temple of God), therefore smoking (for me) is a sin. First Corinthians 3:16 and 17 in the Amplified Bible Version states, "Do you not discern and understand that you the (whole Church at Corinth) are God's temple (His sanctuary) and that God's Spirit has His permanent dwelling in you—to be at home in you (collectively as a Church and individually)? If any man does hurt to God's temple or corrupts (it with false doctrines) or destroys it, God will do hurt to him and bring him to the corruption of death and destroy him. For the temple of God is holy—sacred to Him—and that (the temple) you (the believing church and its individual believers) are."

The perplexing problem that had me in its grip was the tobacco leaf, laced with the enslavement of nicotine. My ability to subjugate the grasp of the incinerate was gone— I was hooked! I had been captivated by a habit my parents had taught me was detrimental to my health. Growing up, and from my own horrid smoking experiences, I also made myself a promise never to get addicted to anything that would dominate and control me.

So, there I was, in the here and now of my life. I was, by the grace of God, living a life committed to His glory. I was a student of God's Word, involved in the life of my church, and purposely telling others about the love of God through

Jesus Christ the Lord. In the natural world's eyes and by outer appearances I had it "going on." However, the truth of the matter was that even though I was living a righteous life on the surface, there was underlying exasperation. It was like a duck on the water. On the water's surface the duck looks calm and restful, but underneath, hidden from view, the duck's feet are in constant motion to stay afloat. I was like the Biblical character Naaman, portrayed in 2 Kings 5:1 (KJV): "Now Naaman, the captain of the host of the king of Syria, was a great man with his master, and honorable, because of him, the LORD had given deliverance unto Syria: he was mighty man of valor, but he was a leper."

Naaman, for all practical purposes, was a man of exceptional success. He was an honored leader among his colleagues and the king. Naaman was an accomplished and victorious leader on the battlefield, renowned for his defeat over the infamous Syrian army. He was known as a brave and accomplished commander of men and a war strategist.

However, even though Naaman was a man of high acclaim and accolade, known by all, no one wanted to be near him to shake his hand The last conjunctive phrase, "but he was a leper," negated all the glorious depictions of his wonderful character. He had a good résumé indeed, one that would get him a job almost anywhere. Naaman would have been the envy of many a man in his day for his great accomplishments. There was much good registered toward him as a good person in his field. It is the same today among the populace of our present times. People are seemingly good, decent, and honorable people, even to the extent of being heralded as righteous.

A person may be perceived as a Christian, Godly in word and deed. However, the Word of God concludes and consigns all as sinners. Romans 6:23 (King James Version) proclaims, "For all have sinned and come short of the glory of God." The operative words are "all have sinned." In earlier verses in Romans, chapter three, the Apostle Paul seems to pronounce the same sentence to all of humanity. In Romans 3:10 (KJV), the man of God declares, "As it is written, there is none righteous, no not one." Then, in Romans 3:12 (KJV), it is further promulgated, "They are all gone out of the way, they are together become unprofitable: there is none that doeth good, no, not one." We are, of a truth, all sinners saved by grace!

So then, like Naaman, I had obtained a credible reputation of being "a good man." It had been a tedious and wearisome expedition, full of continuous ups and downs, ins and outs, comings and goings. Conversely, the people around me witnessed my changed habits and accredited to my name and honor good accolades. Members of my church, my community, and my coworkers had assigned me the status of a righteous man. However much good was said about me concerning my sanctimoniousness, in my heart I knew there was an undeniable "but" to mar it all.

With Naaman, the concluded inscription was "but he was a leper," while with me, the reference could very well have been (among other faults) "but he was a smoker." Both leprosy and my smoking addiction were infirmities of the flesh, and both would require the hands of God for a cure. There are many things in this world that mankind has no solution for. Thank God for His awesome power! Is there anything too hard for God to do? (I am being facetious with this foolish rhetorical question.) The Holy Father and Creator of heaven and earth can do anything He wills. When human faith is coupled with the holy and divine will of God, all things are possible.

Smoking is wrong (at least in my mind) and should not be something a Christian should partake in. I was also told by a few unsaved people whom I was witnessing to that they did not think a Christian should smoke. These two points of view caused an agitation of mind that I was not prepared for. Apparently, neither nonbelievers nor I felt that a Christian should use tobacco, and here I was, a hopelessly and helplessly addicted smoker. How could I be an effective witness to people who did not know Jesus Christ as Lord while doing things that may deter them from hearing my testimony?

The perplexity that challenged me at this time was beyond my capability. I was a confessed Christian with a genuine inclination to live a life worthy of representing my Savior and Lord, Jesus Christ. If smoking a cigarette would damage the effectiveness of my witnessing, then it had to go. I sincerely wanted to win souls to the Lordship of Jesus Christ. I did not want to do or say anything on my part to dissuade anyone from receiving and knowing the One Who could save anyone, the Begotten Son of God.

The Amplified Bible Version of 1 Corinthians 8:13 reads, "Therefore, if (my eating a) food is a cause of my brother's falling or of hindering (his spiritual advancement), I will not eat (such) flesh forever, lest I cause my brother to be tripped up to fall and to offend." I personally perceive "meat" in this valuable verse as representing anything that isn't essential. If there is anything nonessential for my sustenance and is offensive to a Brother or Sister, I am obligated by the mandates of God's Word to deny myself. Apostle Paul addresses this situation (in my interpretation) in his writing in Romans 14:14–22 (New American Standard Bible): "I know and am convinced in the Lord Jesus that nothing is unclean of itself; but to him who thinks anything to be unclean, to him it is unclean. For if because of food your brother is hurt, you are no longer walking according to love. Do not destroy with your food him whom Christ died. Therefore, do not let that which is a good thing be spoken of as evil. For the kingdom of God is not eating or drinking, but righteousness and peace and the joy in the Holy Spirit. For he who in this way serves Christ is acceptable to God and approved by men. So then let us pursue the things that make for peace and the building up of one another. Do not tear down the work of God for the sake of food. It is good not to eat meat or drink wine, or to do anything by which your brother stumbles. The faith which you have, have as your own conviction to God. Happy is he who does not condemn himself in what he approves."

The Scriptures convicted me, other people confirmed me, and my conscience reproved me, all in harmonizing agreement that my smoking habit was against me in the least three ways. First, smoking was harmful to my body, which is the temple of God (a fact that is printed on every pack of cigarettes by order of the surgeon general), and God forbid that I should defile His housing. Secondly, while I had begun witnessing to others of the love of God through Jesus Christ, His Only Begotten Son, my smoking habit was a stumbling block and a distraction. Then, thirdly, the money I was spending on cigarettes could have been used toward family and household needs. And, certainly, the money I spent on cigarettes could also have been used to finance my church and Christian ministries. It was obvious that smoking was a detriment to my life, witnessing, and health—it had to go!

Making the decision to stop smoking was easy, but the effectuation of the stoppage was a different narrative.

Bringing about the cessation of my smoking addiction was undoubtedly one of, if not the most, difficult tasks I have ever experienced. I knew, however, it was something I had to do, and I had to do it immediately!

I announced to my family and church my endeavor in suppressing my enslavement to cigarettes and nicotine. I confessed the hardship of the task and solicited their prayers. When I made public my desire to rid myself of tobacco, it was if I opened the doors to the pits of hell. Satan unleashed riveting strongholds on my tastebuds and body in the urge to satisfy my tobacco needs with a vengeance. It was indeed a trying time of embattlement with the Devil.

Knowing the power of God, I gave myself to much prayer and fasting. I must have aroused and engaged Satan's ire, as my need for nicotine only seemed to intensify. The most critical times were after meals and when I was in the presence of others who were smoking. The irony of it was that even when I smoked, I never liked the irritating odor, but now that I was trying to quit the habit, even the smell became somewhat delightful.

My praying and fasting did not expedite my power over cigarettes as I had hoped. In my impatience, I pondered on what I could do to accelerate the quitting process. When there was no prompt sign in view, an epiphany came to me. It was simple and would be advantageous to my cause.

I had curtailed my smoking greatly, but the fact was I was still smoking. This revelation was the birth of a pathbreaking hope. I made an agreement with my wife that gave her permission to buy a new dress anytime she caught me smoking. The rationale behind this allowance was knowing that our monetary resources could not afford many such actions. This, in theory, would help fortify my self-discipline, resulting in a permanent resistance against the urge for cigarettes. However brilliant the intention, I still smoked. I became disgusted with myself in my inability to refrain from smoking. I found myself, a grown man, returning to the antics of my childhood days. I was "slipping around," smoking in secret, hoping not to be caught (especially by my wife).

After tiring of the "hide and smoke" hullabaloo, I decided to confess to my wife and inform her that I had continued smoking. To my utter surprise, my news was no news to my wife. She notified me that she was well aware of my smoking in secret. She further stated that the giveaways were the antiseptic and mints on my breath. My wife was compassionate and understanding, which resulted in the dissolution of our agreement (my wife initiated the end of our pact—a wonderful woman!). She told me she did not want me to have to sneak around to smoke.

Even though my anti-smoking plan was not successful, I was not giving up. I told myself this was something I had to do. I couldn't smoke and proclaim myself a Christian; it was against my inner constitution. Therefore, I gave myself to other distractions that I thought, hopefully, would ultimately lead to the total elimination of my need for tobacco and nicotine.

I tried to suck on candy as a substitute for the nicotine cravings. When the sugar fix didn't work, I adhered to the well-meaning suggestion of a friend in chewing tobacco instead. This habit was short-lived per direct (and forceful) undertones from my wife. I was abruptly interrupted one night from a peaceful, nocturnal state of rest by a cold, shrill voice. It was my wife using that voice, the one every man in the holy bond of matrimony can attest to. Every man's lifelong partner has at least two voices: one exudes delight, her "Atta Boy!" that lets the man know he has met her good pleasure. Then, there's that dreaded "Uh-oh" voice that expresses her displeasure with her husband in whatever he has done or said. I digress here briefly to share a mystery that has baffled me (and myriads of other men also, I'm sure) for years. A man can amass fifty "Atta Boys!" but one "Uh-oh!" can cancel out all the accumulated "Atta Boys!" A mystery that has yet to be explained from the beginning of mankind until this present, contemporary time.

Getting back to that eventful night, I was awakened by the irritation of my wife's "Uh-oh" voice. I struggled to gather my wits about me as I muttered, "Huh? What's wrong?"

"You're spitting on the wall, that's what's wrong!" she retorted, still using that cutting "Uh-oh" tone of voice.

My night life habits stemmed from my daytime activities. I had ascribed to tobacco chewing as the alternate to cigarette smoking, and therein lay the source of my current nighttime problem. During the daytime hours I chewed tobacco. Unlike other tobacco chewers, I was unable to hold the extractions in my mouth. I spat incessantly; I spat nonstop during the day and subconsciously in my sleep. Needless to say, my tobacco-chewing venture ended that night.

I did some other silly and asinine tactics that I will not take the time to mention, largely because I am too ashamed to let them be known. All that I gained from these anti-smoking demonstrations was the ability to witness of their stupidity and unworthiness.

Time and efforts went by swiftly in my quest to overcome my penchant propensity for smoking. Everything I attempted to do was ineffective in quelling the voracity and hunger for tobacco. I became discouraged and depressed in my failures to dominate my taste for tobacco. I had prayed, fasted, and done virtually anything suggested to me to accomplish my goal. It devastated my mind and spirit, not being able to defeat this stumbling block that hindered my mental and spiritual progress.

Then, the day arrived for my deliverance, and it came through the Word of God. On this glorious day, I had finished my work quota and gone to my known place of isolation, the steel shed. Now, I must make a confession concerning my isolation. I was secretly smoking, concealing the acts from others by strategically positioning myself in a place that allowed me to see any approaching traffic.

I had just finished a cigarette and then prayed to God for strength and guidance in His Word as I read my Bible. On this ordained day I was reading Psalm 43 when verse three seemed to jump out from the page. The verse reads, "O send out Thy light and Thy truth: let them lead me, let them bring me into Thy holy hill, and to Thy tabernacles" (KJV). The request of this man appropriately expressed the sentiments of my desirous petitions.

Later that evening when I did my home reading, I read from Psalm 119. Psalm 119:50 had special meaning for me: "This is comfort in my affliction: for Thy Word hath quickened me" (KJV). These verses in Psalms made me realize that all I needed was in God's Word. His Word was my portal of escape from my afflictions and bondages, all of them.

As I ruminated on these verses, I also mused over some things I indicated in an earlier chapter. I must put Jesus first, hence the question is not "What *would* Jesus do?" but "What *did* Jesus do?" I wanted my actions and words to mirror the actions and Words of the Savior.

It again dawned on me that Jesus always depended on the Word of His Father. Reminiscent of how the Son of

God used Scriptures in overcoming the prowess of the Devil, the thought motivated me to think on this scenario afresh. The synopsis was simple—Jesus used the Word of God to defeat and ward off the Devil.

Jesus stated in John 4:34 (Amplified Bible Version), "My food (nourishment) is to do the will (pleasure) of His Who sent Me and to accomplish and complete His work." John 7:16 (King James Version) says, "James answered them, and said, My doctrine is not Mine, but His that sent Me." John 12:49 (Amplified Bible Version) quotes Jesus this way: "This is because I have never spoken on My Own authority or My own accord or self-appointed, but the Father Who has sent Me had Himself given Me order what to say and what to tell." According to John 12:24 (New American Standard Bible), it declares that Jesus said, "He who does not love Me does not keep My Words; and the Words which ye hear is not Mine, but the Father Who sent Me." Then, in His conquest over the Devil in the wilderness, there were series of "it is written" (the Word of God).

It is my personal conviction and opinion that these verses declare that Jesus Himself relied and depended on the infallible Word of God. Therefore, if Jesus Incarnate (human form) depended on God's Words, how much more should we of fleshly composition read, study, and put to memory God's verbiage of the Bible? In every situation, the attestation of selected verses in Psalm 119 should vitalize and strengthen the believer. Psalm 119:104, 105, and 115 were then and remain invigorating to my mind and spiritual being. (It is to be noted that all readings are from the King James Version.)

Psalm 119:104 states, "Through Thy precepts I get understanding; therefore I hate every false way." In Psalm 119:105 the writer declares, "Thy Word is a lamp unto my feet and a light unto my path." Then, in Psalm 119:15, the Psalmist continues, "Depart from ye evildoers: for I will keep the commandments of my God."

When I thought on these verses, I praised God for the great discovery of His Word He had allowed to come to my mind. It is by His Word that I must take my stand against the Devil and his evil ruse. I am not wise enough nor do I have the strength to maneuver a defense against Satan. The power of God is my fortress in opposition to all nefarious forces. The Word of God is steadfast and will always be there for the defense of a child of righteousness. Jesus said this of the endurance and the conveying potency of His Word: "Heaven and earth shall pass away, but My Words shall not pass away" (Mark 13:31 (KJV)). The Hebrew writer describes the Word of God as quicker, more powerful, and sharper than any two-edged sword.

Thank You, Lord! I have searched the Scriptures and learned how to defend myself against the Devil and his temptations; it was there all the time, but I'm just now getting it! It is so marvelous how the God of heaven and earth will reveal what a person needs to know in deliverance at the precise time of need. Then that person realizes it had been there all the time, but he or she is just getting it! That's why believers ought to be constant and diligent in reading, studying, and meditating on the Word of God. He has given us a wealth of information to empower us in every circumstance. The answer to every problem mankind will encounter is solidified for this life's needs. The only reason a person does not find an answer is because he or she does not ask for or seek a solution. For when a person faithfully and diligently searches for a solution in the Word of God, that person will find that it had been there all the time, but he or she is just getting it.

21
HARD BUT WELL WORTH IT

If there is one thing life has taught me, it's that the accomplishment of success is difficult and tedious, to say the least. As a child, I was often told, "Anything worthwhile doesn't come easy and anything easy is usually not worthwhile." As an adult, I have come to agree with this archaic adage. In taking the cue from Apostle Paul's expression in Romans 14:5c (KJV) to "let every man (person) be fully persuaded by his (or her) own mind," I have made this a personal conviction to live by.

The Bible offers a great deal of verses that validate persistence and staying power. We are challenged to endure to the end, and if we do, we will reap our reward. We are not to throw in the towel just because the road gets hard and bumpy, especially so when a goal or value of recompense is involved. It is a sad commentary that many a person failed to reach success simply because they gave up too soon.

On the subject of persistence or "no quitting," I am reminded of two stories I would like to share:

The first is about a young man, twenty-three years of age, who saw an ad in the newspaper that read, "Wanted—Young Man As an Understudy To A Financial Statistician. The successful candidate must be a hard worker who knows it will be well worth it. All interested persons must send résumés to PO Box 1720, Opportunity, USA."

The young man applied for the job but never received a reply. He wrote again and again and again, but no response came concerning his application. He went to the post office and asked for the name of the company for Box 1720. He was refused this information by both the postal clerk and postmaster, as such an action would be an infraction to federal law.

The young man left the post office in disgust and desperation, since he really wanted this job. He came up with an idea and on the next morning got up early and went to the post office and stood near Box 1720. After long hours of waiting, a man finally came to the mailbox and removed the mail. The young man inconspicuously followed him, who led him to a stock brokerage firm.

The young man entered the building and requested to see the manager. After being asked his reason for wanting to see the manager, the receptionist went into a room behind her desk and closed the door, leaving the anxious young man standing in front of her desk. The receptionist finally came out and instructed him to go in behind the closed doors.

After knocking and being granted entrance, the young man entered the manager's office. The manger spoke to him in a highly agitated tone of voice. "We intentionally did not publicize our name and address, so how did you come about finding out we were the advertisers?"

The young man went on to explain, "Well, sir, I applied for the position of understudy to a financial statistician. I wrote three letters to your firm and never received a response. I also got up early and went to the post office for information but was denied the name of your mailbox ownership. I got up early this morning and stood for several hours watching Box 1720. Finally, a man came in and took mail from the box. After hailing a cab, I followed the man here. Sir, I am truly sorry if I have offended you, but I really want this job and have gone through too much and come too far without going all the way!"

The manager remained quiet with a stern expression on his face for a short time and then replied, "Young man, after all you've gone through, I'm sorry to report to you that the job is filled. However, you are the kind of persistent person I have been looking for. You're hired. Your getting here was hard, and I promise to make your efforts worthwhile."

The other story that emphasizes persistence is about a young boy who wanted to learn to ice skate and one day become a famous hockey player. His parents bought him a pair of skates and took him to the local ice-skating rink. The boy asked his parents to leave him at the rink and he would call them when he was ready to come home.

The boy went through a series of falls and spills. After receiving bruises, a bloody nose, and scraped hands and knees from the constant falling, a sympathetic onlooker approached the beat-up boy and kindly suggested, "Son, maybe you ought to quit and try another sport. You're going to kill yourself trying to ice-skate."

The boy, getting up from the ice on wobbly legs and losing his footing on several attempts, finally got to his feet. Standing gingerly, the boy wiped the tears from his eyes and the blood from his nose, then hobbled to a bench and said, "I didn't get these skates to learn how to quit. I got them to learn how to skate!"

These two stories expressed my sentiments for my situation in life at that time exactly, to a tee. I had come too far and gone through too much to let the habit of smoking stop me. I made up my mind never to have to suffer the humiliation of repentance and having to come before my church again. I just wouldn't let that happen. I wanted to live for Jesus and to succeed in living a life that would allow the world the blessedness of seeing a Christian. Oh, I knew it would be hard, but I also knew the rewards would be well worth it—in this world and the world to come.

Apostle Paul wrote in Romans 8:38 and 39 (Amplified Bible Version), "For I am persuaded beyond doubt—am sure—that neither death, nor life, nor angels, nor principalities, nor things impending and threatening, nor things to come, nor powers, nor height, nor depth, nor anything else in all creation will be able to separate us from the love of God which is in Christ Jesus our Lord."

Then, in Roman 8:34–36, the man of God makes a catalogue listing condemning articles that can be waged against Christians. However, in verse 37, a glorious assurance is given: "Yet amid all these things we are more than conquerors and gain a surpassing victory through Him Who loves us" (AMP).

The matter of addiction was ever before me, front and center. I wanted to stop smoking for a number of reasons. However, the most important reason was, in my heart and mind, because smoking was wrong, especially for a Christian. In addition, I found myself slipping around to do what I felt to be sinful. I gave myself to much prayer and fasting. I also solicited prayer from my family and church members, and tried to end the habit by implementing other substitutions that would hopefully enable me to reach my desired goal.

I must admit this was a trying time for me in every aspect of my life. Satan was invading the privacy of my thoughts by infiltrating my mind with doubt and fear. I became disgusted to the point of asking myself, "What's the use? I'll never make it, I'm a failure!" Even in my Bible reading, it appeared I was doomed and being pronounced guilty. In Romans 1:28 (King James Version), it is written. "And even as they did not like to retain God in their knowledge, God gave them over to a reprobate mind, to do those things which are not convenient."

Had God given up on me? Had God given me over to a reprobate mind? I needed to know the answers to these pressing issues. I cried out to the Lord both day and night, "Lord, please save me! Give me strength to overcome my evil inclinations, please deliver me. I can't do it on my own power."

Again, I continued reading my Bible, praying, fasting, soliciting prayers from others on my behalf, and attending church faithfully, all the while hoping to hear a Word from the Lord. However, there was no Word to be found from any source that would energize me spiritually and raise me out of this horrible pit. No Word from the Lord, but Satan was incessantly whispering in my ear messages of discord, doubt, and fear.

Recognizing that God's timing was not necessarily my timing, I continued on with a determination of faith. I would not listen to the undertones of the Devil. The Words of Jesus kept reverberating in my mind: "Ask and it shall be given to you; seek and ye shall find; knock and it shall be opened unto you." I didn't know what to do to kick this smoking addiction, but one thing was sure. I would be persistent in "asking, seeking, knocking." I would not let Satan get the best of me this time! There was no turning back; I would keep on "asking, seeking, knocking" by faith until I was given an answer, found a solution, and/or the door be opened to me.

This time of my life was filled with anxiety and consternation. Dismay threw me into a state of confusion, leaving me bereft of what to do. I found myself sorrowful to the point of weeping and could not determine the cause of my tears. Bewilderment set in, complicating even my salvation and relationship with Jesus Christ. If I was in Christ and Christ was in me, why wasn't I able to conquer this demon enslavement of tobacco?

There was a war taking place within the confines of my mind. However, even in that disarrayed state of distorted reality I was resolved not to give in to wavering fluctuations. I would be persistent, I would forge forward, there would be no quitting this time. This time I wouldn't allow myself to backslide. Satan, I serve notice on you—I will not be double-minded, feeble-minded, weak-kneed, unsteady, faithless. I'm going through to see what the end will be!

This was not a tranquil period for me, but I continued in prayer, fasting, and Bible reading. I learned to encourage myself through the truth of God's mighty Word. The need for nicotine still demanded to be satisfied, and yes, I was still smoking in secret so as not to offend or weaken another person. This time would be different from all other regressions. It was hard, but I believed that if I persevered, God would make it worthwhile!

I really can't express it adequately in words, and my next statement may be difficult for some to accept. However, sometime later, I can't say how long (but it was longer than I wanted), I experienced a great phenomenon. The Holy Spirit spoke to my inner mind. It was not an audible voice, but an internal, visceral communication. I knew that voice that I heard speaking to me. I knew that voice and was confident in Who it was that spoke to me. When the Lord speaks, the sheep of the Good Shepherd know that voice. A person who has been spoken to by Him will not soon forget the authoritative yet serene tenor and power of it. I will avoid the burden of details in telling of the agonizing trials and tribulations that I went through this disturbing time of my life. I will only conclude it by saying it was troublesome and overwhelming. If it had not been for the Lord speaking to me, I can say with almost one hundred percent certainty that I would have lost my mind or reverted to depravity. I did not want to fall victim to either of these contemptible circumstances.

I was encouraged by the Voice to think on what I had learned about Jesus from the Word of God. Then, it hit me like a bolt of lightning. That was it, I needed to go back to the Bible for answers that would alleviate me from my unpleasant circumstance. Thank God for the unsearchable and inexhaustible riches of His Word!

In rethinking the way of Christ, I remembered that throughout His life and ministry here on earth, He used for His defense the Words of His Father. Whether the nemesis was Satan himself (spiritual) or the Jewish hierarchy regime (flesh), the Lord's methodology was the same—He counteracted their attacks with the Word of God. As I thought on the effectiveness of the Lord's way, I was encouraged to follow Him of Whom I am a disciple. I would arm myself with Bible verses.

After my curiosity regarding Jesus's masterful stratagems in handling the Devil was satisfied, I received a greater spiritual insight. Whenever the Word of God is hurled at Satan as a bulwark of defense, he has to retreat. When one studies the pattern of Jesus, she or he will discover that the resistance Christ employed was always "what thus say the Father." Whenever the Prince of Darkness is confronted with and opposed by the Word of God, he has to retreat. The King James Version quotes James 4:7 as saying, "Submit yourselves therefore to God. Resist the devil, and he will flee from you." Two questions come to mind after reading this verse Firstly, how can a person be in submission without surrendering to His Word? His Word shows a Christian what she or he should do in being a child of God. Secondly, how can a person put up a resistance against the Devil that will cause him to flee? No human has any power, either physically, mentally, or spiritually, to command the Devil to flight. Alone, no human being can accomplish this annihilation except by the power of God's Word.

It was at that time a new wisdom came to me as to what to do in overcoming my smoking addiction. Every time the need came upon me, I would task my mind with memorizing Scripture. So go ahead Satan, attack my taste buds with nicotine cravings. Instead of tobacco, I will use the Word of God to quench my appetite for nicotine. The need for a cigarette will be my push to commit to memory verses from the Holy Writ.

I got a Gideon New Testament/Psalms/Proverbs Bible, the small one (three by four inches) that easily fits in a man's shirt pocket for carrying convenience. I will never forget the first time I replaced nicotine with the Holy Word. A member of my work team lit up a cigarette, and as it would happen, the smoke (I believe Satanically directed) found its way to my nostrils. I immediately removed myself from the area, probably twenty or thirty feet from the fumes, and took out my New Testament copy. Since I have a special fondness for Paul's letter to the Romans, I decided to make this my initial Book for memorization.

When I began my Scripture-memorizing defense against Satan, the desire for tobacco seemed to intensify. I now feel that this increase was orchestrated by the Evil One himself. And then, in my afterthoughts, I concluded also that it may have been caused by God as a test of my faithfulness. Whatever the cause or purpose, I was determined to stay my course in my attempt to ward off the Devil.

Now, lest it be construed as an easy chore, I must hasten to say it was quite the contrary. Satan played havoc with my mind in making me feel worthless when the results were not immediate. I received a new exegesis for Jesus's statement in Luke 21:19 (King James Version), "In your patience, possess your soul." This, one of my memorized verses, is also stored in my mind as recorded in the Amplified Bible, "By your steadfastness and patient endurance you shall win the true life of your souls." It was difficult but I was determined; I resolved to emulate my Savior in patience and using the Word of God in overcoming Satan's evil influences through the nasty habit of smoking.

It seemed the change wasn't coming, but by the grace of God, I pressed forward. Then, miraculously, one day I noticed the frequency in desiring a cigarette lessened. God, eventually, in the span of a few weeks, had given me strength. I no longer had to distance myself from cigarette smoke. In fact, the scent of burning tobacco became detestable to my sense of smell. I was able now to remain in the presence of smokers and try to instigate a conversation about God and His goodness (sometimes successful and sometimes unsuccessful).

Now, when I look back at that time of my life, I recognize and praise God for taking away my addiction to nicotine. It didn't happen instantly (overnight, so to speak) but took a long period of time. I had to memorize most of the letter to the Romans while detaching myself from the presence of others, and even when I was alone and craved a cigarette, it was a period of weariness and hardship. But God blessed me with the power of endurance. Every time Stan enticed me to smoke, I resorted to God's Word for strength, and at the same time, I became equipped to fight the Devil in the same fashion as used by my Lord and Savior, Jesus Christ. As His follower and disciple, like the Master Teacher, I fought Satan with the Word of God.

The distinguishing philosophy was definitely in bringing victory over the Lord of Evil through the utilization of God's Word. I'm convinced that when Satan recognized that his arousal of my need for tobacco drove me to the Scriptures, he loosened his control. It was a long, hard journey, but it was well worth it for at least two reasons. First, I was delivered from the enslavement of tobacco, and secondly, I learned that the Word of God has the power to bring victory in every situation and complication of life. The power is right there in the Word of God!

Just because I was delivered from the clutches of nicotine, it did not mean then, nor does it mean now, that I had a permanent dominance over Satan and his enticements. While it is true I was no longer a smoker, it did not preclude the viciousness in the Devil's attacks. I had won a battle against him by the execution of God's Word, but warfare against the Prince of Darkness was yet raging, trying to conquer my soul on every side.

When I achieved superiority over cigarettes, Satan was quick to supplant other diabolical exchanges in my mind.

I had some unsavory and insipid thoughts that had never crossed my mind before then. The Devil tried to seduce me with appealing allurements that caught my attention. He did it with fascinations that I will not call out in any particular arrangement. I would just like to report that it was a volatile time and leave it at that, please.

I witnessed to a female friend who had smoked for years and tried to stop, but she was too far advanced in the habit. I was able to share my testimony of what God had done for me. I was extremely honest and forthright in explaining the technique God had given me in using Scriptures to nullify the desire for cigarettes. The woman told me she really wanted to quit and that she had tried every available recommendation, including the patch.

I told her of the times I had to separate myself from the aroma of tobacco and steal away alone with my Gideon New Testament copy and give myself to memorization of Scripture. I also shared with her the turmoil of disgust I faced when I didn't progress as rapidly as I thought I should have. I used Scriptures that strengthened me for success in that objective as well as in other successive conquests. I rejoiced in being able to witness to her in how the Lord, through this God-given exercise, had brought me out as a conqueror. I then told her of how I was able to use memorizing the Word of God as the defense against the Devil and his wiles.

My encouragement to her from my mouth was, "If He did it for me, He will do it for you, for God is no respecter of person. Everything that we need is in the power of His Word! I want, though, for you to always keep in mind that it won't be easy, but if you endure, God will grant you the victory!" (This quote may not be verbatim, but the wording is to the best of my recollection).

Some time later (a few weeks), I saw my friend. She greeted me with a big smile, then reached into her purse and pulled out a copy of a Gideon New Testament. The woman reported to me that she hadn't totally quit, but that she had reduced the number of cigarettes she smoked by "a whole lot." She also told me she was proud that she was now able to "spit out Bible verses." I don't know (or even if I ever knew) how long it took, but I do know she eventually overcame the tobacco habit and is now a nonsmoker.

Much later, probably four or five months, when I talked with my friend, she heartily thanked me for sharing my testimony with her. She stated that it was the greatest thing that had helped her to kick the habit, and at the same time read the Bible. She admitted that she was one of those people who went to church but never found the time to really read the Bible. My friend shared with me that she had quit once and then made a commitment to stay faithful for three months in all that I had suggested. She told me that although she had not overcome her smoking habit, she was reading her Bible. She testified that she saw the difference in her life to the point that people asked if she was going to start preaching. She concluded her story by telling me it was as I had told her, hard, but if a person sticks to it, it would work. In that conversation she asked and was granted permission to share the method to a friend. My message to her was that it was not mine and that God gives us gifts that we may pass on to others as a blessing.

Having learned these great truths about God and His powerful Word, I am positive that His Word is more than enough to meet every need of the human race. When I was raised in Malvern ("God's Country"), the older men instilled in us the importance of keeping our word with the catchphrase, "A man's word is his bond." As young men, we were encouraged to keep our word so that if we said something, we would be believed. It may not be possible with humanity to do all we say, since many things can emerge to hinder us altogether from carrying out a declaration. However, with God, no person has to dismay concerning His promises or ability to carry them out. There is no failure in God! How do I know, you may ask? My answer lies in the words of the Christian children's song "Jesus Loves Me" — "The Bible tells me so!"

Many things have transpired since I have been delivered from cigarettes and my smoking habit. However, as I stated earlier, regardless of the number of times a person may be victorious in battling the Devil, he will be back. Rest assured that his departure is short-lived, he's just gone for a season. Satan wants to break the heart of a loving Father by enticing every person who comes to this life by way of the womb, to sin. He is persistent in "seeking whom he may devour" (1 Peter 5:8b (KJV)). All his deviousness is aimed to break the heart of a God Who loves all His Creations all the time.

I praise God that He blessed me to overcome the all-encompassing power of tobacco and nicotine. However, I must stop here to make a confession. I was able to resist in allowing tobacco from reclaiming mastery over me. The stench nauseated me whenever I was in the company of people who were smoking. Strange as it may seem, there were times the aroma of smoke brought delight to my nostrils and taste buds. I actually considered bumming one of the fiery sticks just to see how it would taste and make me feel. Yeah right, Satan! Just to see how it would taste and make me feel, and most likely get me addicted again. Thank God for His Holy Spirit Who brought back to my mind that verse that says, "Flee the very presence of evil." I got away from the temptation, thereby preventing spiritual mayhem. God's Word succored me in escaping this snare.

There were other instances when Satan attempted to captivate my soul with unscrupulous and sinful suggestions. I will not take time to write on them, only to state that they were many and often. It got to the point that the hellish insinuations were so strong they caused me to despair. There were times when they were so hard for me I almost lost hope and confidence. The worst came from the Master of Deception in making me question my salvation. He fed my mind with doubtful inquiries—*Why am I having these thoughts if I am a Christian? Why are these ungodly entrants in my mind? Why am I even thinking on these evil temptations?*

This was a devastating time for me. I didn't know how to get rid of these evil thoughts and desires. In truth, I was not always successful in denying the lust of the flesh. I satisfied some of the pernicious cravings of my body by committing acts that I knew were not pleasing in the sight of God or man. Furthermore, I have to confess that I was well aware of what I was doing while engaging in these acts of sin. I fell short of the glory of God by giving in to sensual and devilish allurements. Satan enticed me through sensual fascinations and the false security of thinking no one would see or know about it. Here I was again, gone back to depravity where I had vehemently declared never to return. I was depressed and hurt as the Devil told me there was no help for me and I was forever a hopeless, helpless, and incurable hypocrite.

I was near giving up and resigned myself to being what I was—a wretched sinner! Distress and dejection had absorbed my thoughts to the point that I was too tired to care anymore. In this low state I found myself crying out, "This is it, I can't do it! It's too much for me, I might as well follow my mind and have some fun!"

Then, there was a small, still voice (or better yet, a burning sensation) within me that spoke in a voice of authority. The Holy Spirit brought to my remembrance what I had done to obtain deliverance from the bondage of tobacco and nicotine. "That's it!" I cried out. "I must use the Word of God as I have in the past!" I felt the urging of the Holy Spirit to consider the things that had allowed me former spiritual victories over Satan and sin.

I did a lot of praying, fasting, and thinking during this unsettled and disturbed time. After a period of intense meditation, I concluded that God's Word is powerful and sufficient for all situations of life. If God's Word can be potent enough to strengthen me in conquering a smoking addiction, surely it can be effective in all other undesirable behaviors. Jesus did say that heaven and earth will pass away but His Word will always stand (Matthew 24:35). If Jesus's Word will endure the foundations of heaven and earth, undoubtedly His Word would be sufficient for all my needs.

I ventured out on my new inspiration to fight any and all of Satan's onslaughts. I will not give extended details in how I executed God's Word in these contentions of my life. My testimony is simply stated in the accumulation of my many temptations, ups and downs, depressed and exhausted times. Through it all, I am happy to report that God delivered me from every situation. I remained in prayer, Bible reading and studying, and memorizing Scripture. It is amazing how when a person commits Scripture to memory, the Holy Spirit miraculously brings them to mind at the precise time they're needed. My conclusion is that there is power in God's Word for answers to every conceivable (and unconceivable, for that matter) circumstance.

There is power in God's Word and when used wisely, it

can protect the believer against evil forces. However, I must hastily remind you that it involves exhaustive measures of prayer, Bible study, and memorization. It is not easy, and to be honest, it will put an exacting strain on the mind, body, and spirit. Candidly speaking, it is a complexing and draining discipline that will actually drive a person to spiritual delirium. The process requires mental fortitude, physical stamina, and the spiritual endurance of Job. The person who strives against the wiles of the Devil must also possess faith, hope, and a long-suffering spirit. It is hard, but if a person puts the Word of God as their safeguard against evil influence, she or he will find it all well worth it.

In all that I have been able to overcome in this life in the way of sin and temptation, I have come to the conclusion that if God brought me through "this," he can bring me through "that." I used God's Word for every consequence of life that crossed my path. It came to me that if God's Word could bring me victory in overcoming the hardest compulsion I had ever come across (or had ever come across me), my smoking habit, it could achieve victory over all other possible pitfalls.

I apply God's Word in every phase of temptation that comes before me. There is plenty of Word to be used in the defense against evil and vile seductions. I am more than convinced that God's Word is all a person needs to ward off Satanic attacks of lustful desires that go against the way of the Lord. Since my deliverance from my smoking dependency, I have been able to use this same methodology for all the Devil's other allurements. I am thankful to be able to broadcast the truth of my doings; it has worked every time! Every time I needed to overcome the chicanery of the Devil in his attempts to bring me to spiritual decline, the Word of God succored for me a victory. Everything a person needs is in the Word of God!

Many years have passed since these times. I have testified to a vast number of people who have been harassed by sinful inclinations that were either bothering them or had entrapped them. Whenever I was aware of a person's desire to quit smoking, I was spontaneous in sharing my triumph over the habit. I also gave to many the testimony of my success via God's Word in overpowering sinful temptations and lust that appealed to the weakness of my flesh. Always, purposely, I made known to those I witnessed to of the hardships of the method I proposed. The message was the same to all: "It's hard, but if you endure, you will find that it works and will be well worth it!"

Some tried my suggestion but afterward found it didn't work for them. However, when we discussed the experience, it was obvious that they really hadn't wanted to go through the process. After all, as I have stated throughout this book and always testify to those I share with concerning this way, it is not an easy fix. The way I have found appropriate for every circumstance involves patience, endurance, and fortitude. However, if a person is inclined to completely and faithfully follow it through, she or he will find it profitable and well worth it!

There are a few who later thanked me and shared the success(es) they gained. I supposed if I compared the number of those I know to have tried, endured, remained, and persisted with those who fell by the wayside without receiving the blessings of the process, I could very well be discouraged. I know that giving God's Word an indelible place in one's mind works. Thank You, Lord, for the few who, along with me, have found that this way is hard, but well worth it!

The writing of this book is inspired by personal events that I declare to be factual, true, and proven. I pray that God will bless anyone who reads my words to be motivated to undertake the method conferred in my testimonies. I certify that if fully maintained, the person will overcome the contrivance of Satan and weaknesses of the flesh. The toiler will find triumph in life and enjoy remarkable growth in familiarity with God's Word.

I would like to end my writing with a story, with the hope that it will convey the simplicity of all I have striven to put into print. The story goes:

With his son going off to college, the last thing his dad did was to give his son a Bible with the instructions, "Son, read your Bible. Everything you'll ever need is in it!" The father reiterated this thought to the son repeatedly in the few moments before each bid farewell and the son drove away.

The son tucked away the Bible in a bag as he left to begin his life as a college man. The son got so involved in the party life and the college scene that he never found time to read his Bible. The boy had every intention of reading his Bible as he had promised his father, but he was so busy having fun that finding the time was nigh impossible. The son would console himself by saying, "I'll read it tomorrow," but tomorrow never seemed to come.

However, in the second year of his schooling, the young man incurred financial obligations and his car needed to be repaired, which called for more funds. The son called home and informed his father of his difficulties and his need for money, only to hear his father give him religious platitudes. The father simply said to his son, "I see you haven't been reading your Bible. I told you, son, everything you need is in your Bible—it's in the Word of God!"

All I Need Is In God's Word

The young man was in need of money. This was not the time to open the pages of the Bible and read. He was desperate, and this was all he could get out of the old man. The son had also gotten behind in his college obligations. He called home and each time he talked to his father, it was always the same, "Son, I told you to read your Bible. Everything you need is in your Bible—it's in the Word of God!"

Seeing that he was not getting anywhere with his father, the young man solicited the help of his college dean, asking him to call his father to explain his situation. However, the father's answer was firm. "Tell my son to read his Bible. Everything he needs is in his Bible—it's in the Word of God!"

The dean reported the results to the young man. "I spoke to your father, but I'm afraid I had no success in reaching him either. He only kept telling me all you need is in your Bible, and asked me to encourage you to read a book I don't believe in."

Weary and highly agitated with his father, the son finally, out of desperation, picked up his Bible and randomly flipped through the pages. The son was amazed by what he saw and shouted out, "Dad was right! It's here, it's all here! All I need is in the Bible, it's all there in the Word of God!"

The father had placed hundred-dollar bills between every page in the Bible, and on the last page was a blank check in the son's name. There was even more than the son needed, and it had been there all the time. It was in the Bible, it was in the Word of God!

May God bless all to know that all we need is in His Word!

ACKNOWLEDGMENTS

I thank God for affording me the opportunity to put my growth testimony on the printed page. God has allowed me the power of continued spiritual maturation and retention in His Word to defeat Satan and sinful inclinations through the flesh.

I am grateful to my wife, Tina, for her offer to do the typing. I refused the offer only because I wanted to reword and reedit as I typed and received the inspiration. Thank you, sweetheart, for proofreading, suggesting, and critiquing for a better way of expression.

I also would like to thank my friends who kept asking of the progress and completion of my writing. Your inquiries made me industrious in finishing the work. I will not put into print those names lest I overlook anyone. However, thank you from the bottom of my heart for your encouragement and prayers.

ABOUT THE AUTHOR

Billy Blackmon has been preaching the Gospel of Jesus Christ for over fifty years. He pastored two churches (in Hot Springs, Arkansas, and Topeka, Kansas) for a total of twenty-nine years. He was also a welder, welding instructor, and Hospice Chaplain.

Billy attended secular and Bible colleges where he earned a bachelor's in Christian Ministry, a master's in Religious, and a doctorate in Christian Counseling.

Billy and his wife, Tina, love traveling and are committed to doing for as long as their finances and health will permit. He loves Arkansas and has the personal aphorism, "I was Arkansas bred, and when I die, I'll be Arkansas dead!"

www.ingramcontent.com/pod-product-compliance
Lightning Source LLC
Chambersburg PA
CBHW020524080526
44583CB00013B/726